This Book Is For You If...

- You feel conventional skill-building doesn't work for you. Does it feel that sometimes it actually takes you backwards?

- You've given up on particular goals because you just couldn't find a way through.

- You sometimes find yourself thinking that positive thinking isn't particularly positive. And sometimes it looks more like denial.

- You feel so stuck that you don't have the energy to take even the first step forward. Maybe you've been going two steps forward and one step back, or even one step forward and two back.

- You wonder how some people seem to have natural motivation. It seems as though someone forgot to tell you something crucial that would make life so much simpler - and more fun.

- You wonder why you're working so hard and still not getting to where you want to be.

- Occasionally you've been 'in the zone' and experienced effortless success. Now you'd like to learn how to find your way there more often.

- Sometimes it feels like life prioritises you instead of vice versa.

- You've had success in one area but not been able to repeat it in other parts of your life.

About Kieran O'Connor

> It's not the daily increase but daily decrease. Hack away at the unessential.
>
> BRUCE LEE

In his late twenties Kieran experienced a period of overwhelming stress; he went through a time when he was emotionally, mentally and physically exhausted. It was like running on an almost flat battery that all the sleep in the world could not recharge. He felt so stuck that it seemed that no matter what he did he wouldn't have the energy to cope with the result of his actions. In leverage terms, he had too many problems and not enough solutions in his life.

Although it was a very difficult experience, these days Kieran describes it as a timely wake-up call and a valuable lesson. For one thing he learned to ask for help and eventually booked in to see a psychologist who specialised in work-related stress. Therapy was useful for a while, but Kieran felt it was missing something... "How will I know when I am back to full health?" he asked one day and the psychologist looked blankly at him as if he had never considered the question before.

This was the **tipping point** that inspired Kieran to educate himself on how the mechanics of the mind/body connection really worked. As an engineer who could fix just about anything, he decided he'd make incremental changes in his life and observe the effect of each change. One switch he made over the years was from Shotokan Karate to Wing Chun Kung Fu. As much as he loved the former, the latter contained more of the balanced mindset that suited him. It contained a 'sweet spot' with the yin aspect of being able to flow like water yet also the yang striking dynamics that are associated with the short distance explosive power made infamous by the late Bruce Lee.

Another key **pivotal moment** for Kieran was the study of Transcendental Meditation. One day, about two years into his daily practice, he'd finished a physical workout and was still wearing his heart monitor as he went into a meditation session. On this one particular day he had an experience that he cannot easily identify; all he can say is that the data from his heart monitor showed that he'd gone as low as 28 beats per minute. He was a very fit guy so had a regular resting heartbeat of around 50 but this experience was nothing to do with fitness; it was more based upon tapping into an altered state of consciousness. It felt both heavenly and, at the same time, totally normal. It was like being halfway between heaven and earth. This deepened his interest into the intricate workings of the mind/body.

He realised that perhaps not everything is as it seems. For example, could it be possible that all of his 'problems' were created by his own willingness to habitually continue doing the things that did not truly work for him day after day, week after week?

The time he spent in that profound state of body and mind gave him just a tiny glimpse into the depths of his subconscious and he began to see into its secret places.

Although this peak experience eventually melted away, he retained the idea of how past habits draw on us in the present day, like being stuck in a big pair of boots in deep thick mud. He understood that the harder you try to fight your way out of a habit, the less you succeed, but this conflicted with what he had been brought up to believe - that working hard always pay dividends. How on earth could both of these ideas be true?

It was this puzzle that sent him on a long journey around both the hemispheres of the world and of the mind and it eventually resulted in the creation of this book. The answers and ideas you find within these pages may sometimes seem too simple...but those simple truths are the seeds that lead to real and lasting change. Including...

What is the secret to a more fulfilling life?

Day by day, do more of what already works for you and less of what doesn't.

Why Invest In Leverage?

1. Tried, tested and proven ideas on getting more of what you truly want in life more of the time.
2. Use science-based knowledge to get out of your own way.
3. Enjoy more success more easily, more often - and still have time to play.
4. Learn what works for you and then invest your valuable time in these activities.
5. Get used to seeing simple solutions where you used to see complex problems.

What Sets This Book Apart?

The Little Book of Big Leverage is unique. Here are some of the reasons why:

- It helps you tap into your existing motivation even if you don't know you have it yet.
- It builds on your existing skills even if you don't know you have them yet.
- It combines both scientific principles and everyday common sense.
- It provides tools and drills to help you wire in the improvements.
- It helps you build on your gains even after you have finished the book.
- It's reverse engineered from techniques that really work by a professional chartered engineer.
- It integrates over 30 years of martial arts study, practice and experience.
- It offers a balanced approach between Western-based sciences and Eastern philosophies.
- It works on both your conscious and subconscious mind with principles, concepts, metaphors and examples.
- It activates your ability to recognise and then use leverage more easily, more often.
- It frees you from the trap of trying to solve a problem from the same mindset that got you there in the first place.

Note: This is not a book on positive thinking! That is a great example of 'trying to solve a problem with the same thinking that got you there in the first place'. This book will however assist you in taking positive action.

THE LITTLE BOOK OF BIG LEVERAGE

THE ART OF RELEASING THE RESISTANCE
to tap into your natural flow

KIERAN O'CONNOR

Published by
Filament Publishing Ltd
16 Croydon Road, Beddington, Croydon,
Surrey, CR0 4PA, United Kingdom.
Telephone +44 (0)20 8688 2598
www.filamentpublishing.com

© 2017 Kieran O'Connor

The right of Kieran O'Connor to be recognised as the author of this work has been asserted by him in accordance with the Designs and Copyright Act 1988.

ISBN 978-1-911425-17-5

Printed by IngramSpark.

This book may not be copied in any way without the prior written permission of the publishers.

A portion of all book royalties will be donated to wateraid.org

Contents

Acknowledgements		11
Preface		15
Part -1	Introduction	19
Part 0	**The Nature Of The Mind**	**35**
	Chapter 0.1: Natural Learning	37
	Chapter 0.2: Autopilot And RAS Function	43
	Chapter 0.3: Delayed Gratification	47
	Chapter 0.4: Updating Habits	53
	Chapter 0.5: Perceptual Filters	57
	Chapter 0.6: Conscious And Subconscious Alignment	61
	Chapter 0.7: The Spring Clean Effect	65
Part 1	**The Eustress Filter (Initiating Leverage)**	**69**
	Chapter 1.1: Ideo Dynamic Leverage	71
	Chapter 1.2: By The Power Of A Pause	79
	Chapter 1.3: What You Can Measure You Can Improve.	85
Part 2	**The What Works Filter (Transitional Leverage)**	**95**
	Chapter 2.1: The Elaborate Elusions	97
	Chapter 2.2: Finding The Hypnotic Path Of Least Resistance	111
	Chapter 2.3: Harnessing Habits	143
Part 3	**The Purposeful Practice Filter (Momentum Leverage)**	**155**
	Chapter 3.1: You Become What You Practice	157
	Chapter 3.2: Compounding By Design	167
	Chapter 3.3: Even While You Sleep	175
Part 4	**The Leverage Activation System (LAS)™**	**189**
	Chapter 4.1: The LAS™ Cycle	191
	Chapter 4.2: Making Practice A Practice	203
	Chapter 4.3: Reminding Your Mind	213
Part 5	**The Final Hypnotic Instalment**	**221**
	Chapter 5.1: Reverse Engineering Our Way Back	223
	Chapter 5.2: Compounding Your Gains	229
	Chapter 5.3: Leverage Your Future	243

Illustrations

1. Learning And The Nature Of Problems — 38
2. Immediate Versus Delayed Gratification — 48
3. Leverage Perceptual Filters — 58
4. Conscious Versus Subconscious Mind — 62
5. Yerkes-Dodson Law — 73
6. Levnosis Attitudes — 115
7. Daoist Habitual Model — 158
8. Compound Interest Example — 169
9. The Four Levels Of Waking States Model — 179
10. The Spiral Effect — 193
11. The Leverage Activation System™ (LAS) — 196
12. The Practice Model — 204
13. The Ebbinghaus Effect — 214

Experiences

1. Watching Wally — 28
2. Elastic Zone Exercise — 75
3. Eustress Versus Distress — 89
4. Fractionation Mode And Defractionation Mode — 123
5. Engage Your Autopilot Mechanism — 130
6. Engage Your Automicity Mechanism — 133
7. Saddle Up Your Trojan Horse — 151
8. Engage LAS Lite™ — 194
9. Re-Engage LAS Lite™ — 199
10. Engage Weekly Recognition — 233
11. Engage Monthly Reward — 236
12. Engage A Yearly Picture — 238

Acknowledgements

The list is so exhaustive that I will just capture the key characters here.

To my amazing **mum and dad** to have always encouraged me in everything I have done in life whilst also trusting me enough to learn my own tough lessons. Teaching me that falling, scraping our knees and then getting back up are all part of the risks in improving the quality of life has been invaluable through both the ups and downs. Your support has always been incredible. Love you beyond words!!!

Another special thanks to **Andy and Liz Torelli** in Newport Beach, California who out of the blue offered me a space in their beautiful ocean view home over Christmas and New Year 2014/2015 to complete the first outline of this book. Without their support, this book might have stayed firmly on the runway and never gotten off the ground. The hospitality and kindness of you both, your wonderful family and your fantastic friends was totally off the scale. I'm forever grateful.

Jane Mallin not just for her fantastic skills as an editor but also for going the extra mile with her intuitive guidance. She cracked the whip as well as giving such kinds words of encouragement and this has allowed me to not only pull this book together, but also learn a tonne from the experience. Your gentle patience amazes me.

Lastly, I wanted to thank all the teachers in my life. Whether at school or university, martial arts, in engineering, seminars, books I have read and so many more. A huge heartfelt thank you to each and every one!!!

Kieran O'Connor
August 2016

> Give me a lever long enough and a fulcrum upon which to place it and I shall move the world.

ARCHIMEDES

Preface

 The hurrier I go, the behinder I get.

LEWIS CARROLL

Generally speaking, the modern world has encouraged us to place such an emphasis on doing that we have to a degree lost touch with our sense of beingness.

People get so caught up in the hustle and bustle of their everyday life that they inadvertently carry over habits that take up their valuable energy while bringing little or no benefit. We tend to spiral downwards if we are not aware of this as the more fatigued we become, the more time we spend on habits that make for poor investments. I use the word 'investments' as what we do today always brings dividends tomorrow, even if those dividends bring more bad than good. As time goes on and the days roll into weeks, weeks into months, months into years, little things gradually escalate. Ever lost your temper over a tiny thing because you let a situation build up until you reached breaking point?

Think of a habit that doesn't work for you; now imagine a penny or a dime. If you added a coin to your pocket every day you indulged in the 'bad' habit, it wouldn't take long before the weight became noticeable and eventually started affecting your energy levels. Is it any wonder that so many people feel fatigued? Now think of one of your good habits that do work for you while still imagining a coin. Imagine utilising these coins in a different way. Rather than carrying them, they go into a savings account. They in essence become part of your reserves.

If we are to bring about more of the latter, we need to shift our perspective. As an example, traditional Chinese medicine has a strategy that has withstood the test of time. The focus is on restoring balance as a priority to assist in bringing the body and mind into alignment. This supports the body's natural healing ability and thus allows energy reserves to naturally do their job. Some Chinese medical practitioners following the old ways will prescribe, say, a 12-week Chi Gung class rather than immediately reaching for the pills. Chi Gung is a very intelligent system of physical exercises that use an external physical movement to help correct an inner loss of balance. For example, a person with diabetes would be given some exercises that would assist with their pancreatic health and efficiency. Another person with high blood pressure is given exercises to gently help their nervous system gradually and incrementally release tension. After the patient has finished their course, the doctor is then able to prescribe them a much less potent drug or even a clean bill of health.

The doctor helps the patient educate themselves on good self-care and so assists their longer term health rather than just focusing on the reported problem. Education is the underlying principle that allows the doctor to assist the patient in taking responsibility for their own well-being.

The word 'education' can bring up a whole spectrum of responses. Many of these will depend on how a person experienced their school days, which fall during the most formative stages their development. This spectrum covers anything from stories of having teachers who inspired them greatly all the way to the other side where schooling was very much a punishment-based experience.

I missed quite a bit of early schooling for a number of reasons and always felt I was playing catch up. However, I recall several teachers who really cared about their role and were willing to go the extra mile to help me.

The middle stages were a bit of a mixture, many of them the typical ones that an adolescent male experiences when passing through the testosterone stages of development. This led to a dilemma. Do I focus on being smart or do I focus on being athletic? There didn't seem to be a middle ground. In addition, my formal education seemed to be too much about learning for the sake of learning with not enough focus on what happens out in the real world. It felt like there was a disconnect between schooling and earning.

In the later stages of learning, I fortunately found a way to strike a balance between the formal education system and my job in the field of design engineering. I did a part-time engineering degree in Edinburgh and made a deal with my employers that I would stay with them for at least three years after completing the degree so they would also benefit from the qualification. All they had to do was to be flexible with my working patterns to assist my studies so that I could achieve the demands of reaching the qualification. This win-win scenario meant that once completed, I would have leverage over the people who had opted for purely education or purely work. It was an incredibly tough challenge to undertake but an investment that would go on to pay huge dividends.

Looking back, I believe that it was very much my introduction to martial arts at the age of 12 that created a shift for me and allowed me to start to discover, piece by piece, a way to integrate the formal education system with real world application. Martial arts gave me a glimpse of the Eastern mindset and a fresh perspective on 'how things work' that seemed more **fluid in nature**.

Fluidity in the East is so often represented by the nature of water and we will tap into (pun intended) how we can discover more of our own nature via the skill of **re-establishing balance**.

Bringing us back to the present day, I believe that here and now, there is a great opportunity in this modern age to blend the ancient wisdom of the East with the modern science of the West.

When you integrate and blend these two, you will experience a fulcrum point that will bring you the best of both. You will find yourself in your flow more often and more naturally such that a state of super fluidity will replace any old need to rush and push your way through life.

> We cannot solve our problems with the same thinking we used when we created them.

ALBERT EINSTEIN

Part -1

Introduction

No, you didn't misread the number above. I've used minus one deliberately because we need to build solid and deep foundations so that the rest of the material will flow more easily as you progress through this book. This introduction may take up a bit more space than usual but that's because I want you to be able to do something unusual - make lasting, beneficial changes.

My Mission Is To...

1. Help you learn how to make your mind work for you by integrating your conscious wants with your subconscious habits.
2. Assist you in regaining your natural enjoyment of learning - and to do that as naturally as possible.
3. Use the nature of leverage to help you feel more in flow with life more of the time.

This Book Aims To...

1. Be a handy toolkit that helps you get unstuck whenever you need it.
2. Provide conscious understanding while utilising subconscious communication.
3. Tap into the wisdom you've gained from your life experiences. You may see some of these experiences as good and some as bad, but I hope you'll come to see them all as infinitely valuable.

Once Upon A Time...

...there was a painter and a sculptor who both took an interest in each other's work. The painter was baffled by how the sculptor could work with nothing in front of him, no sketches or photos on which to base his art. At a stretch, the painter could paint what was in his head but only did his best work when he was drawing from life and transferring that image onto canvas.

"How do you do it?" he asked his friend one day.

The sculptor pondered a while. He said, "I don't create a sculpture as such. It's more that I uncover the form bit by bit." Then he quoted the man whose work and perspective he respected the most:

> " Every block of stone has a statue inside it and it is the task of the sculptor to discover it. "
>
> MICHELANGELO

He saw his talent as being able to patiently wait for the potential within the stone to reveal itself and then inch by inch, bit by bit, chip away at the rough edges. He'd simply and lovingly take away the parts that did not belong. To him, the beauty of the finished article was always there; it was just covered up and only needed his assistance to bring it into realisation.

This book will help you use the chisel of your inner discernment to chip away at what you carry around that doesn't align with your true nature. This mismatch is the source of every problem you currently perceive.

Where Eastern Wisdom Meets Western Science

In the last century, brilliant scientists such as Albert Einstein and David Bohm helped us move on from the traditional Newtonian paradigm while still respecting what it helped us gain at the tangible level of physicality. As we progress into the world of quantum physics, science is finding more and more links with ancient cultures. Daoists revealed thousands of years ago what modern scientists are coming to realise today. I believe that as time goes on we will see more alignment between scientific evidence and ancient wisdom. They already share a common theme: that everything becomes more truthful when broken down into its **simplest** nature. This is where chipping away at what doesn't belong becomes so useful.

Three Daoist concepts are particularly helpful when we want to keep things simple. These are the foundations that this book stands on:

1. Separate And Combine

The Daoists were not just expert learners; they also knew a thing or two about learning how to learn. They could see the elusive obvious - learning is a series of breaking things down and putting bits back together in a certain order. It's not so different from building muscle through weight training. The resistance applied causes minute tears in the muscle fibres which connect back together during rest to create larger muscle fibres.

The way we learn is no different; we use new information (resistance) to break down the present structures that we know. We then create new understandings which are a combination of what we already knew plus the additional information. We assimilate information by filtering what is offered to us. We either agree to let the new information become a part of us or we reject it, at least to a degree.

Through their systematic practices, the Daoist masters saw that there was a huge imbalance between what we consciously learn and what we learn at a subconscious level. They could see, for example, that a student learned less from what was purposefully taught and more from just being around the teacher. It was as if the unspoken mastery was the most important factor in shaping the student.

Such subtleties of the human mind are often overlooked, however modern quantum science has helped us begin to re-evaluate them. One example is the infamous Double Split experiment. From this came one of the most discussed

> Daoist masters saw that there was a huge imbalance between what we consciously learn and what we learn at a subconscious level.

premises of quantum theory which has long fascinated philosophers and physicists alike: 'by the very act of watching, the observer affects the observed reality'.

A documented study in Nature (International Weekly Journal of Science, 26th February 1998) reported on a highly controlled experiment performed at the Weizmann Institute of Science. The experiment demonstrated how a beam of electrons was affected by the act of being observed.

Professor Mordehai Heiblum headed a team who constructed a device measuring less than one micron in size, which had a barrier with two openings. They sent a current of electrons towards the barrier. The 'observer' in this experiment wasn't human. Institute scientists used a tiny but sophisticated electronic detector that could spot passing electrons. The quantum observer's capacity to detect electrons could be altered by changing its electrical conductivity, or the strength of the current passing through it.

Electrons at the submicron level, when behaving as waves, simultaneously passed through several openings and then met again at the other side of the barrier. This created a pattern described as interference.

Although it didn't follow scientific expectation, the interference only occurred when no one was watching. Once an observer began to watch the particles going through the openings, the picture changed dramatically. It was noted that if a particle could be seen going through one opening, then it was clear that it didn't go through another. In other words, when under observation, electrons were somehow influenced to behave like particles and not like waves. Therefore at this subtle level, the mere act of observation affected the experimental findings.

To return to Daoism, the idea of 'separating' is the idea of breaking things down to their simplest states so they could take a measure of control over their destiny. It is very clear in Daoism that as beings, we are influenced by so many factors that control is somewhat of an illusion... But the ability to observe means that we do have an influence on where we want to take our lives.

To separate anything, first we have to be able to observe what it is we want to break down so we naturally tap into the observation effect when we engage in the art of change.

We can see that just the act of observation has the ability to create change. If we are always changing just by the process of awareness, how can we tap into this to improve the quality of our lives?

2. The Water Method

The Daoists described two main models of progressing in life: the fire method and the water method.

The fire method uses force and struggle. This is not to be derided or ignored. We all know that there are times when we really have to push ourselves. It's more that we want to save this for an emergency so we work smart and reserve this approach for when we really need it. It shouldn't be our usual way of getting things done.

The Daoists have a great respect for fire and I have witnessed this first-hand. In China, at the top of Wudang Mountain (the Mecca for Daoism) there is a shrine with a memorial flame which is supervised by a Daoist master 24 hours a day 365 days a year. The flame has burned for more than six centuries. When I witnessed this flame, I was amazed at how many Chinese would make the demanding journey to spend time with it. The flame seemed to symbolise a connection to those who had already passed on from this life. So fire is very much respected when used wisely within an appropriate context.

> Nothing is softer or more flexible than water, yet nothing can resist it.
>
> LAO TZU

The water method emphasises flow and following one's own nature; it's the way the sculptor at the beginning of this chapter worked. He'd respectfully chip away at the parts of the stone that did not belong. The water method aims to allow the individual to discover what works for them in life while letting go of what doesn't.

Stress increases as the pace of life accelerates. In the modern world, people are working longer and harder even though technology was meant to alleviate our workload. We've also been sold the belief that if something isn't working for us we can't be trying hard enough. Is it any surprise that people's best efforts so often end up with them getting even more entangled in the problem?

We have to lose the one-size-fits-all mindset too as it has the unfortunate effect of making people look outside of themselves for answers. It borders on craziness to think that because something works for someone else it must work for us too. But it's a very common belief in our 'civilised' society.

Rites of passage played a big role in tribal societies. They marked the transition from childhood where other people's opinions were most important to adulthood where your own opinion of yourself was the priority. We have long since jettisoned those rites of passage and many of us seem to be stuck in a perpetual adolescence where we seek to fit in with others. Yet we also want to be free to be ourselves. This sets us up for an ongoing conflict which is actually an illusion because humans free of confusion always seek a win-win scenario where the individual's needs are in harmony with the environment. With the water method, it is possible to find that path of least resistance.

3. The Problem Isn't Where You Think It Is

The truth is that if you know what the problem truly is you cannot have the problem. You will only see the solution.

We live in a world of cause and effect yet are generally not so good at separating the two. We so often confuse the trigger of what we experience with the underlying cause. We often find, for example, that a problem started further back than we initially imagined.

We only notice the problem when it escalates to a point where we can no longer ignore it. But we're so overworked and overstimulated that even if we see the problem, all we will do is react to it, which leads to us getting even more enmeshed in the problem. The term 'can't see the woods for the trees' describes this reactive or autopilot mode. When we have sufficiently rested we are more able to respond and therefore more likely to find a solution.

During Easter 2015, the £14 million Hatton Garden raid, believed to be the biggest burglary in British history, hit the headlines. The heist was well publicised not just because the gang members were mostly made up of old age pensioners but also because if it was not for the modern-day CCTV technology that allowed the police to piece together the means, motive and opportunity, they may have never captured the cunning culprits. Criminal experts showed, for example, how the thieves passed under the general public's radar by counter-intuitively wearing hi-viz clothing. The thieves knew that people in the vicinity of their operation would generally be on autopilot - which means they're neither paying attention to their surroundings or thinking about it - and so they can't identify a thief especially if the culprits are wearing something that obviously makes them stand out from the crowd. It is as if people are automatically programmed to see thieves as caricatures wearing black balaclavas and carrying swag bags. Autopilot therefore switches off awareness and acuity.

As we progress, we'll learn about the dynamics and nature of the mind to a useful level. Not too simple and not too complex. We'll aim at just enough to help gain a measure of control over the autopilot state. As we gain a level of skill and awareness, we'll see more clearly where we inadvertently get in our own way and create problems for ourselves.

> Knowing others is wisdom,
> knowing yourself is enlightenment.

LAO TZU

This book also offers a way to tap into the modern wisdom of what is termed 'hypnosis' which is simply the study of the dynamic nature of thoughts and emotions that divide our conscious awareness and subconscious habitual nature. We'll gain more understanding about our habitual nature and we'll find a fulcrum point where we have one foot in Eastern Wisdom and the other in Western Science - together these two bodies of knowledge can help us see through the illusions associated with having your autopilot...on autopilot.

The Hypnotic Elusive Obvious

The Elusive Obvious was a term coined by Moshe Feldenkrais, an Israeli physicist and the founder of the Feldenkrais Method, which was designed to improve human functioning by increasing self-awareness through movement. Feldenkrais applied his judo expertise and his scientific skills to become a leader in the field of human performance and achievement.

His most well-known publication was the book *The Elusive Obvious* which dealt with the simple concept that we operate from a set of fundamental ideas that, through habit, become elusive to us.

Most of the things which bring us problems in our lives, the mistakes, hardships, and suffering, have a simple cause. It's when we live today with the same rules, habits and deeds that we used yesterday and still expect them to be applicable today. The reality is that what was a good habit yesterday can make us unhappy today.

But we are a species that knows how to learn and learning means that we can change with everything we learn. Obvious as this is, it is an elusive truth. People in general habitually lack free choice because of their investment in their habits. This cycle of buying into the delusion of 'no-change' is what eludes the truth. It is therefore an elusive truth that people generally lack free choice, yet they're convinced otherwise.

When a person opens up to the idea that each day they wake up they are not the same person as yesterday, the elusive becomes more obvious and informed choice becomes more available to them.

> When someone accepts that each day they wake up they are not the same person as yesterday... informed choice becomes more available to them.

The question for those seeking alignment with their true nature is, 'how can we have the willingness, courage, skills and tools to make what is elusive more obvious?'

When people usually think of hypnosis, they either imagine someone laid on a therapist's couch and an elderly and bespectacled guy swinging an old silver pocket watch from side to side leading the person into a sleep-like state. Or perhaps they picture a stage show hypnotist who has volunteers barking like a dog for the entertainment of the audience.

Within these two extremes lies a place where hypnosis is simply the understanding of various states of mind and body connection.

We all have a conscious mind and a subconscious mind. The conscious mind deals with what we are aware of and the subconscious deals with what we are not aware of. This is obvious...I hope you would agree?

Whenever we learn something, what ever is that we were not originally conscious of then moves across into our conscious awareness. Some things we learn are completely new to us. For some readers the term Elusive Obvious may fit into this category. Some things we already knew but they'd slipped into the recesses of our memories. So learning can also mean reminding ourselves of things once learned; i.e. we bring them back into conscious awareness.

When our conscious wants and desires are in alignment with our subconscious habits, we cannot experience a problem. A problem is an indication of a conflict leading to a form of pain. Now please realise that I'm not making light of the difficulties people face - it's just that there is a difference between physical pain and psychological pain. Physical pain is a basic part of life whereas psychological pain is more contextual. The individual will feel more pain or suffering when they have inner conflict and most inner conflict is really ourselves arguing with the reality we are currently experiencing.

Let's say someone loses their job. If it's sudden, it can be a hell of shock - and the greater the shock, the more they feel it physically. People respond differently to situations like these. While some may feel a total loss of confidence that affects them in the long term, others deal with it with a more matter-of-fact attitude: 'okay, I've lost my job. What shall I do now?' This person's conscious and subconscious minds are more aligned. They are able to harness their resources faster and see solutions more naturally because they see the situation through the eyes of their own true nature.

We will look more at the relationship between the elusive obvious and the dynamics of hypnosis as we progress so that we can align more and more with our true nature. The term that I like to use to describe this phenomenon is 'coherence'.

Coherence: (From Dictionary.com)
    logical or natural connection or consistency.

As you learn more about coherence, it'll seem so simple and obvious that you'll probably wonder why you didn't get taught about it at school.

Leverage - The Dynamics

Leverage: (From Dictionary.com)
1. The action of a lever, a rigid bar that pivots about one point and that is used to move an object at a second point by a force applied at a third.
2. The mechanical advantage or power gained by using a lever.
3. The use of a small initial investment, credit, or borrowed funds to gain a very high return in relation to one's investment, to control a much larger investment, or to reduce one's own liability for any loss.
4. Power or ability to act or to influence people, events, decisions, etc; sway:

Being the only industry in town gave the company considerable leverage in its union negotiations.
Synonyms: advantage, strength, weight; clout, pull.

Let's have a look at these four more closely...

1. The Action Of A Lever... Levers surround us, we use them all the time: e.g. scissors, bottle openers, the handbrake on your car and doors. Door handles are placed as far away as practically possible from the door hinge (fulcrum/pivot) to make for easy opening. If you try closing a door by pushing on a point closest to the hinge, you'll get a sense of how much more effort is needed if you don't have leverage.

Levers are so much part of our everyday life that we would find it very inconvenient, maybe even impossible, to manage without them.

2. Mechanical Advantage. Usually, we're unaware of leverage and only become conscious of it when we have a problem to solve. For example, when I recently tried to remove a screw from the wall, it had such a worn head that the screwdriver could not make a clean connection. One option was to cut the screw and leave part of it in the wall. The other was to risk some wall damage and use a claw hammer to pull out the screw. I had some filler that could complete the repair so I went ahead with the hammer solution. I found that the screw threads were so good at their job in holding the screw in the wall that I had to move my hand to the end of the hammer where the most leverage could be found. I also had to be very mindful about the leverage action and carefully ease out the screw bit by bit. If I'd done it too quickly, the sudden release of energy could have led to me falling over and half the wall coming away.

The mechanical advantage gained by levers was made much clearer to me when I stumbled across an American called Walter 'Wally' Wallington. Wally, a retired construction worker, was curious about how ancient civilisations were able to move massive stones that were so large, heavy and cumbersome that they'd even present a challenge to today's technology.

Wally's website gives some of his ideas about how leverage allows a single person to move massive loads. The simplicity of Wally's ideas are just as impressive as the loads he moves single-handed and it's possible that such methods were used by our ancient ancestors when they constructed such impressive landmarks as England's Stonehenge.

> **EXPERIENCE 1:** WATCHING WALLY
>
> I highly recommend watching some of Wally's footage. Options include:
>
> 1. Access via my website http://www.Findingthefulcrum.org
> 2. https://www.youtube.com/watch?v=uYQBDhkBfr0
> 3. Or go directly to Wally's website http://www.theforgottentechnology.com
>
> In this case, a picture really is worth a thousand words; when I watched it for the first time I began to wake up to the true power of leverage. Why not take a look for yourself and see what you think?

3. The Use Of A Small Initial Investment... Investment has negative connotations for many people, perhaps because of events such as bailouts of financial institutions or because of bad investments they've made themselves. The truth is that even if you've never gone near the financial markets you probably have made some bad investments. The trouble is that people are so often on autopilot that they unwittingly invest in their problems. Sometimes they even become authorities on them. People who spend too much time on autopilot don't get a chance to slow down enough to see what is really going on for them. I'm not judging anyone by the way! I'm on autopilot too. We all do our best at every moment given what we know and what we've learned up until that point. This is a fact and not a fallacy. The fallacy is that if we try harder, we will somehow gain the ability to travel back in time, know then what we know now and get a better result.

4. Influencing Ability. Modern mind sciences have been able to use technologies such as neuroimaging, including PET scans, to help us understand more about how our minds and the structures of the brain operate. Part of this endeavour is about understanding just how much the conscious mind is outweighed by the subconscious mind. One way to see that imbalance is to picture an iceberg. The conscious mind is what we can see above the water and the subconscious is what is unseen below the surface. However, as the scientists continue to learn more, it seems that this old metaphor is no longer accurate. The true ratio is infinitely greater and more like this: one iceberg above the surface is the conscious mind. The subconscious mind is akin to what is below the surface for **all the icebergs that exist in all the oceans.** Judging by this it would seem that affecting the subconscious mind is an impossible task - that is, until you add the power of leverage.

The most foundational form of leverage is awareness; we cannot make anything without it. Awareness is the leverage between the conscious and subconscious, between the volitional nature of the conscious mind and the habitual nature of the subconscious mind. It is the relationship between these two aspects of the mind that makes for the quality of our decisions.

Parts 1, 2 and 3 of this book build on each other. Part 1 is about initiating leverage, Part 2 looks at changing from one state to another, and Part 3 is about building on and accelerating those changes. I think of Parts 1, 2, and 3 as phases: initiating, transitional and momentum. Think about a seesaw that's tipped to one side. Add enough weight to the other side to unstick it and get things started. Then add more weight to bring it into balance. We can also adjust those weights to favour the other side. We will utilise these three phases to help clarify the natural leverage dynamics between the conscious and subconscious mind.

What's Inside The Remainder Of This Book?

Now we're coming to the end of the introduction, we can discuss a little more about the mysterious power of the subconscious mind before moving onto Part 0 which will look at some aspects of the mind that can help you as you begin to apply and integrate the information in the rest of this book. This book aims to show you how to use leverage to tap into your mind so that you can make the most of your precious everyday life.

I am rarely surprised by what the breakthroughs in modern science reveal about the way the mind and body works. Amongst the countless examples that have caught my attention over the years, two stories come to mind that I would like to share with you now.

The first goes back to 1982 when Angela Cavallo lifted a 1964 Chevy Impala off her teenage son, Tony, who'd been working on the car's suspension when the jacks failed and the car fell on him. This case from the USA was so well covered by worldwide media that it drew a lot of attention from the scientific community.

Science tells us that when we are under duress, the hormone adrenaline binds to adrenergic receptors on our muscle tissue causing actin and myosin - the proteins responsible for muscle contraction - to bond faster. Adrenaline also increases the respiratory rate, which raises blood pressure and makes our heart pump harder and faster. Our muscles can be five to 15 percent stronger in these conditions. We are limited, though, by our genetic capability and our muscle development. It's possible that adrenaline removes some inhibition too and gives us a quick burst of strength. However, none of the scientists could explain how Angela lifted that car.

> Maybe we intuitively know that despite our human frailties we are also capable of great things.

There are in fact many stories of this phenomenon. Perhaps it's why so many of people of all ages are drawn to the Marvel superheroes. Maybe we intuitively know that despite our human frailties we are also capable of great things.

The second story I'd like to share with you doesn't include any physical feats but it's an amazing example of how, with the right support, children can overcome negative expectations.

Tony Buzan is a British-based mind expert who developed a tool called Mind Mapping in the 1970s. I had the luck to learn Mind Mapping on a training course when I was working for a pharmaceutical company which had a philosophy of thinking outside the box. The technique became so useful that I still use it today. In fact, each section of this book was mind-mapped when I was trying to transfer the ideas from my head onto paper.

Some years after completing the training course, I stumbled upon a TV programme where Tony Buzan appeared. It was about a group of teenage schoolchildren who had been categorised as 'challenged'. This is a kind way of saying that even the basics of reading and writing were probably beyond their capabilities. Tony offered to work with the teenagers to see if the modern mind sciences could assist them.

The programme showed how Tony was able to shift and adapt learning ideas to each of the child's needs and circumstances. In the finale the children put on a show for the school's other children, teachers and parents and the aim was to display just how much they'd learned and changed as a result of Tony's intervention. The teachers in particular got far more than they'd expected as each child demonstrated one example of their newfound abilities. The most memorable for me was a boy who had struggled with his memory in the past. When his turn came, Tony whispered an instruction in his ear and he quickly left the school hall while the audience wondered what was going on. He returned about 10 minutes later and proceeded to write a series of numbers and letters on a board at the front of the hall. When he had finished, it was revealed that he'd written down the number plates of each and every car in the car park - about 30 cars in all. This was tested as the parents and teachers randomly provided their details. As you might imagine, the level of disbelief was matched by the look of confusion on the faces of everyone who'd thought that such a task would be impossible for even the most gifted children, never mind one who the schooling system had almost given up on.

Science talks of us using only a small percentage of our brains and these two stories suggest that this could be because we're trying to force our minds to do something that is not in alignment with its true nature. Yet when we are in tune with that nature, we are capable of much more than we may ever expect.

Instant gratification (which we will discuss only briefly here) is a great example of where the mind is not being used effectively. Yet it is almost too obvious for most of us to notice when we are doing it. Wanting to be rewarded before we have truly earned something creates confusion and misalignment in the mind. If a seed is sown and disturbed daily to check if it has grown, it won't do as well as it would when it is trusted to follow its own nature and grow.

Delayed gratification is key to the understanding that our current lives didn't happen by accident: they are as they are because of the seeds that were sown in the past. We are always living on the fruits of our past choices whether they were ones that worked well for us or ones that worked against us. This is great news because now we know that if we invest in aligning more with our true nature, nature itself will fulfil its duty to bring us a more satisfying quality of life.

We touched earlier on the field of hypnosis and now I'll expand on it further. The methods and techniques of hypnosis become clearer as the mechanics and dynamics of the brain are more fully charted. Interestingly it is the world of advertising that has made great strides into what hypnosis is truly about because it makes for good business.

One example is the billboard advertisements around the pitch at sporting events at the end of the twentieth century. This is an effective way to advertise as the public watching the event make an association between the sport, their favourite sports people and the product being advertised. This happens almost 100% at a subconscious level - and this is the place where advertising is most powerful. In the twenty-first century, static billboards are being replaced with LED-type technology. Television cameras are set up partly to suit the advertisers, who want to keep their logo and product in the viewers' peripheral vision as much as possible. These moving pictures have an even greater effect on the subconscious than the static billboards ever did.

Advertisers have paid mega bucks to discover how to influence us. However we will use hypnosis for quite a different purpose; we want to de-hypnotise ourselves. We need to wake up from autopilot.

I will now introduce you briefly to a term called automicity. If you look for this word in a dictionary, you won't find it. It came to me in a dream. I had been looking for a way to make a simple and effective distinction between when we are on autopilot and when we are not. I asked my subconscious to come up with a word and when I woke up 'automicity' had surfaced.

Being on autopilot most of the time is not just useful but imperative for efficiency and effectiveness. Airline pilots use autopilot devices extensively to allow them to rest in the air so they can save their energy for take-offs and landings.

The problem with autopilot is that if our lives are too busy, we can end up in a state of mind where our autopilot is itself on autopilot. Then little problems start to grow and, because of the busy mind not being able to see the woods for the trees, we end up with life eventually having to give us a not so welcome wake-up call. All big problems are little problems that have simply been left to their own devices. They only become noticeable when they're allowed grow over a period of time.

This book provides some insights into both Eastern wisdom and Western science which over the years seem to be growing closer together, especially with the progress being made in quantum physics; perhaps one day they will unite within a common ground. Together we will go on a journey through the mechanics and dynamics of mind that relate to leverage where leverage is simply when we are able to tap into the flow of what works for us both collectively as a society and as individuals. My intuition is that you already know how it feels to be in your flow (which is why you are reading this book) but might not be conscious of how it came about. Working together, we will make that state of flow more accessible so you can choose when to enter it and use it to regulate your everyday life.

In Part 0 we will begin the journey of seeing what is already - and always - right in front of us.

Recapitulation of Terms

Separate and Combine - Seeing learning as a series of breaking things down and putting bits back together in a certain order, over and over.

The Water Method - Progress where flow and following one's nature is the primary consideration.

Hypnosis - The study of the dynamic nature of thoughts and emotions that divide our conscious awareness and subconscious habitual nature.

Coherence - Natural connection or consistency.

> There is nothing more deceptive than an obvious fact.

ARTHUR CONAN DOYLE

Part 0

The Nature Of The Mind

In the Introduction, we touched on some areas of the human mind and how, in leverage terms, we want to align our conscious wants with our unconscious habits as much as possible. We've already started to see how hypnosis can offer us a way to assist with this alignment. We'll now look at seven areas that will further our understanding of the mind's nature so we're better prepared to tap into hypnosis so that our mind will work for us rather than against us much more of the time.

Chapter 0.1

Natural Learning

Leverage of the mind's dynamics is fundamental to how we think, learn, behave, make decisions and achieve. Our mundane experience of leverage is often unconscious to us and only becomes conscious when we use it on a physical level. For example, when you brush your teeth you probably don't think about the leverage action of your elbow that brings the brush to your mouth. The skill is taken for granted.

I once got quite a serious hand injury after volunteering for a demonstration on how pressure point techniques in martial arts can effectively subdue an attacker. The risk is that injuries can occur when you make demonstrations as close to real-life encounters as practically possible. My thumb ligaments were damaged for about six weeks during which time I had to brush my teeth with my non-dominant hand. This meant that brushing my teeth took about ten more minutes than usual and I had to learn how to brush them all over again. It showed me how much I'd taken this simple skill for granted all my life.

So how can we take some measure of control over unconscious dynamics of the mind so that we can apply leverage and improve the quality of our lives?

First, it's worth taking a look at what Rita Smilkstein PhD describes as The Natural Human Learning Process (NHLP) in her book *We are Born to Learn*. Rita provides the following definition:

Learning = growing and connecting neural networks.

This may appear obvious as learning and growing seem to go hand in hand. But don't dismiss it because of that - remember the 'Elusive Obvious'?

I believe that problems and learning (or rather not learning) go hand in hand. The following illustration offers some ideas about this relationship. This will be expanded on in various ways as we progress.

FIGURE 1

Learning and the nature of problems

1. A problem occurs when we consciously realise we have not learned a lesson that life and our true nature has offered to us.

2. We only become conscious of a problem when it has occurred more than once.

3. If we naturally learn what has to be learned from each life experience, we cannot experience a problem.

4. All problems therefore are the result of a lack of **natural learning... repeatedly.**

I sometimes wonder why learning so often receives such a bad rap when it is simply a natural process of connecting neural networks. What is it about learning and education that can bring up resistance in people of all ages? Well, I believe that one of Rita Smilkstein's earliest experiences in the educational system might offer us an insight.

Rita's first high school role was a one-year assignment for a class of 12-year-olds and she was to discover that these kids were not an ordinary group. For a start, the class of 18 actually had only two 12-year-olds in it. The remainder of the class was made up of the school's 'problem kids' and the age range was 13 to 17. Plus they were all boys. As you might imagine, she was somewhat intimidated by the stature of these boys who were more like young men. In that particular US state, the education system had to school them until they reached 18 and they would have to repeat a year if they didn't pass it. As I'm sure you have already figured out, some failed year after year. The pupils would eventually be allowed to leave the schooling system at 18 and then, just like the boys in this class, they would be deemed somebody else's problem.

Rita initially did her best to bring the class to order by following all the ways she had been taught in her teacher training but the more she pushed and punished, the more disorderly the boys became. She quickly reached her wit's end. She couldn't envisage surviving a whole year of this. So she started asking the more experienced teachers for advice. They told her just do her best to keep their volume down so at least the remainder of the school could get on with its work.

Ready to give up, she decided to test one last approach. She invited her class to learn whatever they wanted to learn as long as they learned something. She brought in a pile of magazines that would appeal to them, such as ones about sports and fast cars, and placed them in front of the class.

Then she made the class an offer. They could move their desks back to the rear of the classroom and read the magazines and they could even talk amongst themselves just as long as they kept the volume down. If they genuinely wanted to learn something, they could move their desks towards her.

When she made the offer, the boys looked like rabbits in the headlights. It was if she was speaking to them in a foreign language.

She thought that maybe they were feeling as though she was putting pressure on them to make an instant decision. Perhaps they wanted to discuss the offer with each other first. So she told them that she would turn her back for a while to allow them to make up their minds.

She turned her back and there was a silence, a shuffle of desks and chairs and then another silence.

When she turned back around to face the class, she was expecting to see most of the desks at the back of the room with perhaps one or two of the 18 having taken the risk to move towards her. To her amazement, each and every desk had moved towards her. They then openly shared how they really wanted to learn the basics of reading and writing but they knew that they were in this class for one reason and one reason only; to be moved on through the system that had already given up on them. They simply didn't count.

As you might imagine, there were a few tears before Rita was able to get on with the job in hand; finding out how she could adapt to their needs to learn as naturally and rapidly as possible.

As she got more curious about their backgrounds and family lives, Rita noted a common trait. Each of them had no experience of having being read to in their home environments. There were a variety of reasons for this; some parents were immigrants to the US and didn't yet have the ability to read in English while some parents couldn't read at all.

So her first job was to read to them all kinds of stories and to her amazement, they were completely absorbed. Rita continued her natural learning approach and adapted her teaching to what the class needed to engage their minds and allow their creativity to flow. Her primary focus was on what these boys could teach her about learning.

As an example, Rita noticed how during lessons it was common for pupils to look at what the others were writing down. In an examination environment this of course would be considered 'cheating' and could not be condoned. But in the classroom she could see that looking at what another child had written was simply a request for assistance. She then played with the idea of the pupils grouping together in twos and threes to share what they had learned. It became very clear that their learning abilities significantly increased from learning from each other.

In her classroom, learning became an activity that brought people together rather than something that made the boys feel even more isolated than they already did when they walked through those school gates each morning.

Even though these young men had previously had a huge amount of resistance and resentment to learning and the education system, they were now growing day by day. When they were genuinely invited to learn instead of having lessons forced on them, they showed their natural openness, creativity and enthusiasm.

As Rita often says: **"Remember; you are a natural-born learner."**

Rita's invaluable and inspiring story reminded me of my early and very positive experiences at school. My curiosity was insatiable and opening a new book was almost as exciting as opening a Christmas present. But as school progressed my excitement about learning turned into boredom and learning began to feel like a tedious chore.

The formal education system was too rigid and emphasised remembering facts and figures at the expense of more interesting areas such as learning how to learn. Although I appreciate that developing a good memory is both important and useful, education should be about more than memorising endless facts. We're taught facts rather than how to think; we're trained to receive rather than to engage our minds. We learn how to follow instructions rather than solve problems. So what do you do when you've not been given a direct instruction on how to solve a problem? Problem-solving is fundamental to everyone, yet education rarely touches it.

In the long-term, self-sufficiency is more effective than more passive behaviours. Several charities discovered this truth in recent years when they changed how they supplied food and water to drought-hit areas. Rather than continuing to give water to locals for example, the methods and technology for finding water were taught instead. Learning mining techniques and even condensation techniques for taking water from the cold night air has meant that the people are able to become more self-sufficient. You may have noticed at the front of the book that a portion of the proceeds of this book are donated to WaterAid, so thank you for supporting an organisation that helps people genuinely help themselves.

Thankfully, I have rediscovered the same excitement and enjoyment of learning that I naturally had in early childhood. Writing this book is one example of that rediscovery in action.

Go to my website at www.findingthefulcrum.org and you'll find it focuses on the idea that when we tap into natural learning we all have the potential to recover a natural enjoyment and enthusiasm for it. The leverage part of learning will become clear as we begin to understand how a happier relationship between the conscious and subconscious mind allows for learning that is more about flow rather than force. Just as water naturally finds its own path, a mind that is in alignment is naturally able to learn.

Learning flows more naturally when someone understands the general learning dynamics that we all have in common, plus the ideas, concepts and principles that work best and feel most natural for them. By the end of this book, you will be able to select some of the concepts and ideas shared here and apply them in your life. Some of the concepts won't be a perfect fit for you, so just set them aside while seeing that they could be ideal for someone else.

Chapter 0.2

Autopilot And RAS Function

Some would say that 'human nature' is perhaps better and more accurately described as 'human habit'. This is for good reason - we wouldn't achieve much if we had to relearn how to dress ourselves, brush our teeth and feed ourselves every day. But habits can work for us or against us. They can make life better or they can lower our quality of life.

Automation technologies have hugely improved parts of our lives. For example, most long-haul flights use autopilots to help the pilots rest in between take-off and landing, the phases that take the most focus and concentration. By conserving the pilots' energy, our skies are a lot safer. We will touch on this analogy again later when we look at autopilot in much more detail. Industries like car manufacturing use robotics to complete the manual tasks freeing the human workers to focus on final inspections, where a skilled eye is best.

Autopilot starts to become a problem when the autopilot itself is put on autopilot. What do I mean by that? Perhaps this personal and slightly embarrassing anecdote will help you see what I mean. It still makes me smile when I think of it today. I was driving home from work one beautiful Spring evening, which was memorable in itself because the sun rarely makes much of an appearance in Scotland. It was so warm that I had both car windows wound down and it was one of those days where the radio kept playing my favourite tunes. Life felt so good that I could have kept on driving. I eventually got home and pulled onto the driveway, wound up the windows and was just about to switch off the ignition when the penny dropped - I'd moved home four months earlier and didn't live here any longer. Fortunately the new residents were not at home. I stealthily reversed out of the drive and hoped none of my old neighbours would see me... Of course, I've blown my cover now by sharing it here. It's worth it though because this is a good example of my autopilot being on autopilot - I expect you can think of one or two examples from your own experience?

An autopilot is not a way to displace one's responsibility (i.e. the ability to respond). It is a way to manage our energy, efforts and habits in a way that's similar to delegation. Proper delegation aligns tasks and duties with the person who is best placed and skilled to see them through. It can also be used to train someone up to the next level. So delegation is more about the right person, in the right place, doing the right thing even though that 'person' may sometimes be a form of automation or artificial intelligence.

Our current autopilot needs a reset because it too often robs us of our joy and success and ability to tap into natural learning. We want to use our valuable autopilot skills to do more of what works for us and improves our lives.

Dr Maxwell Maltz, a top US plastic surgeon, brought one aspect of autopilot to our attention. He called it the 'servo-mechanism' but it has become more widely known as the Reticular Activation System or RAS for short. While he was a practicing surgeon, he noticed that some of his patients would go under the knife and afterwards acknowledge the change and be happy to move on with their lives. Others however would experience only a brief moment of satisfaction before simply shifting their focus onto the next imperfection. Although the latter clients were great for business, he did not want people facing the risk of surgery in the attempt to meet some ideal of perfection that would always remain out of reach. He realised that their desire could not be satisfied via plastic surgery as their self-image and self-worth were the underlying issues.

Each and every function which we perform consciously or unconsciously is done by some part of the brain. The Reticular Activation System (RAS) is one of the most important parts of our brain and has great influence over our cognition abilities. Recent neuroscience studies related to mammalian brains have demonstrated that this system performs lots of cognitive functions that are related to awareness.

This system is considered the brain's attention centre and the intersection for many functions, including that of motivation. The RAS involves a complex neuron collection that acts as a convergence point for signals from the interior environment as well as from external surroundings. The RAS is a place where your thoughts, internal feelings and outside influences converge. It is very skilled at producing dynamic effects on the motor activity centres located in the brain and the cortex activity such as the frontal lobes which link into our survival instincts.

Other functions include the regulation and shift between the sleep state, wakefulness and how and when we dream. It is also responsible for supplying integrated filtered responses to outside stimuli through **deleting, distorting** and **generalising**.

This helps to make sense of Maltz's experiences with his patients' obsessive focus on the perceived imperfections that are a part of everyday life.

> The RAS is considered the brain's attention centre and the intersection for many functions, including that of motivation.

We've all had some experiences with RAS. For example, after working in Norway for a number of years on my most demanding design engineering contract, I considered that after all the hard work I would treat myself to a Porsche 911, my dream car. Then a close friend passed away and any final hesitations dissolved as I considered how short our time is on this planet. I started my search for the exact model I wanted, which took some months as it wasn't that common...or so I had thought. After I bought it, I was delighted by the engine's purr and the way the car could adapt to the testing road conditions of Scotland as if it had been specifically designed for them. Then suddenly out of nowhere there were Porsches like mine everywhere. What on earth was going on? I finally realised that nothing had changed except that my RAS was now tuned into recognising them. What had been filtered out was now no longer filtered out.

I told a friend about this and she had an experience of her own to share. She'd bought an expensive pair of exclusive designer shoes and soon after spotted another woman wearing the same ones at a distance that would test the vision of a hawk. It's amazing how RAS can give you the pinpoint visual precision of a top-notch military sniper.

Chapter 0.3

Delayed Gratification

Delayed gratification is fundamental to a healthy and balanced state of mind. It is a fulcrum point for investing in a higher quality of life. I first learned of the concept of immediate versus delayed gratification from *The Road Less Travelled* by M. Scott Peck. It was quite an aha moment as it helped me understand a lot more about how people enjoy being rewarded adequately for a proportionate amount of effort.

Too much or too little can be okay now and then but not all the time. A balanced and productive mind can only thrive long-term on rewards that are proportional to effort.

People operate on a spectrum of gratification, with immediate at one end of the scale and delayed at the other. The scale could represent different lengths of time that separate the effort expended from the reward received. The measure itself is based on whether a person would prefer smaller immediate rewards or a larger reward later on (See Figure 2 below).

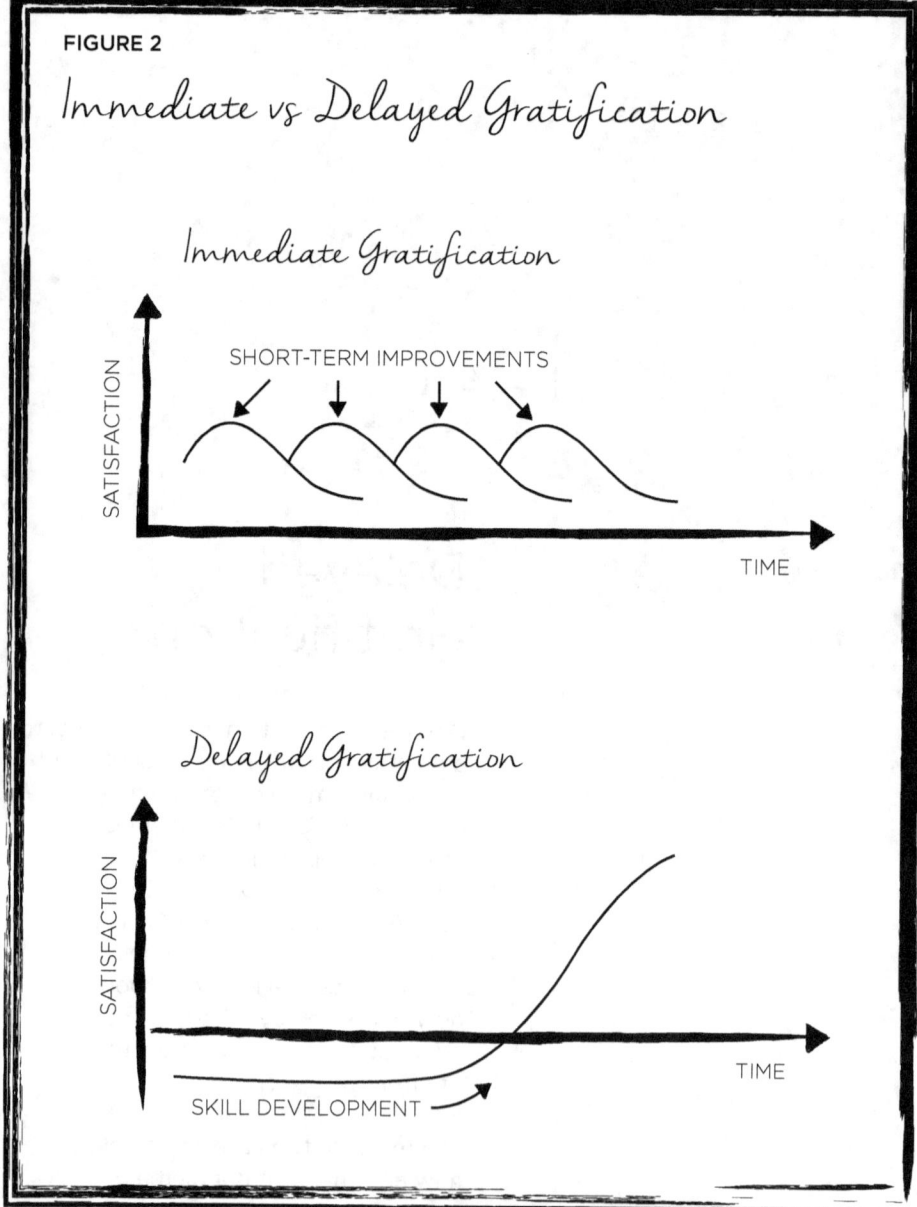

In the 1960s and 1970s, Stanford University conducted its famous marshmallow experiment which received a lot of media attention as it gave an intriguing insight into the dynamics of the reward circuitry of the human mind.

The experiment was based on a group of four-year-olds who were told that if they could wait some time they would receive two marshmallows, but if they wanted and couldn't wait, they could just eat the one in front of them. The person leading the experiment would leave the room and the children were observed and filmed through a one-way mirror.

There was a scale of varied results. Some children would devour the marshmallow as soon as the door shut, while some waited patiently for the observer to return and showed no signs of having to fight an inner battle against temptation. Many of the children had to distract themselves from the tempting marshmallow and they used a variety of tactics to do so, including humming, singing, covering their eyes and even hiding under the table to avoid the marshmallow's influence.

This test of self-control and willpower was made all the more interesting by a number of factors including:

1. **Reliability of the tester:** The experiments were adapted to measure how much the children's responses were affected by multiple tests. For example, if they successfully waited for the adult to return, the adult did not provide the two marshmallows as had been promised. Once they'd been let down, the children would be less likely to delay gratification in the next test.

2. **Follow-up findings:** The children that were able to wait and negotiate the rewards were termed 'high delayers'. The highly documented 20 and 40-year follow-ups on the children revealed some very interesting data that even surprised the academics. Consequence versus reward evaluation ability demonstrated that the children who had naturally been able to delay gratification by their own means - whether by willpower or distraction - were more successful in education and later life. In adult life, the high delayers were shown to be less likely to have addiction problems such as drugs and weight concerns, and fewer of them got divorced.

The experiment's findings demonstrate something that is already known intuitively: when children are taught values such as earning through their own efforts and saving for something they desire, these values become habits that prove repeatedly successful over time.

Delayed gratifications skills can be taught from an early age and it is worth doing so because those early years have such a strong influence on later life.

Examples include:
- Receiving rewards for completing chores especially those over and above what they were expected to do.
- Parents matching the money that their child saves.
- The badges you earned if you were in the Boy Scouts or Girl Guides. They were true badges of honour as they showed you had successfully learned a new skill.

Reliability Of Gratification

If a child is to learn to defer gratification then a lot depends on their teachers. As the Stanford experiment shows, once the child's trust is broken then they are more likely to stop delaying their rewards. Their teachers have to keep their word and follow up on their promises so that the child trusts they will do what they say. It's worth remembering at this point that many of our most important teachers don't work in schools because a lot of our learning happens unconsciously. For example, no one teaches you your accent; instead it's picked up from parents and the people around us and makes us to some extent part of a common tribe. Even those of us who speak in Received Pronunciation like BBC newsreaders had to pick up that accent from somewhere.

Was your trust broken when you were learning about delayed gratification? Perhaps your teachers or parents confused you because they didn't always keep their promises or maybe you spent some of your childhood in survival mode. This would naturally drive you towards more immediate gratification as a habit. Trust for authority figures is critical and these early experiences may easily be underestimated or misunderstood when evaluating a person's ability to delay their gratification.

Even as adults, we experience people who say they'll do something but then not do it. It doesn't usually take too long before that person gets branded as untrustworthy in our mind.

Making deals is an important aspect of survival. A key part therefore of learning delayed gratification is about testing the boundaries of those around us. One area where I've noticed this is in the military when friends have told of the bonding phase they go through in basic training. When people have to rely on those around them to keep them from harm, they tend to test each other very skilfully even if they don't consciously know what they are doing. Teasing and pranks are a huge part of this where the individuals within the unit are tested as to how they will handle stressful situations. These pranks subtly test for character weaknesses that will need to be worked on if their team member is to be fully accepted and trusted.

Later, we will learn how to tap into our ability to discern what works for us as individuals versus what to let go of that might work for others, just not for us. What we will discover is that when we align ourselves with the natural work/reward dynamic, we'll be able to get out of our own way. We'll begin to trust our own nature - and once you experience that, you'll want to experience it more and more.

Chapter 0.4

Updating Habits

Some believe that a habit can be broken. This is a myth. Natural Learning teaches us that an experience leads to the growth of a dendrite which strengthens with time and repetition or deteriorates over time because of a lack of repetition or reminding.

So, given time, a habit can be lost but it can't be broken or forcefully evicted from your life. Forcing will actually make it stronger. But you could always replace a bad habit with a different habit.

Armed with this information, it'd be useful to review the habits we've developed and test them for validity.

What we tend to find is that most of our habits are very useful and support the quality of our day-to-day lives. A number of habits however are not useful but are so slippery and engrained that we continue with them because we don't know how to find a way out.

We will look at how to discern our habits in much more detail later. For now, just bear in mind that when we find a habit that doesn't work so well, we have the opportunity to look for a new habit that is better for us. As the new habit is mindfully applied, the energy that feeds the old habit is gradually removed. Then comes the 'convincing phase' which is a midway point between the old and new habits. The person has reached a tipping point where the old habit gives the last bit of resistance before it finally makes way for the new one.

Let's have a look at the skill-building process, which is a way of taking a measure of control over the move from old habits to new ones. We can then focus on skill-building as a skill in itself that allows us to create more and more useful habits. The new skill is practiced until it has stronger and deeper dendrite connections which will make it feel more natural.

There is a four-step competency-building process that can help us understand the changes that we typically experience when we move from an old habit to a new one.

The Four Stages Of Competence

This model has been attributed to many thought leaders, including Abraham Maslow, however it has been known about in Daoism for thousands of years. It seems that the model has been re-worked a number of times.

By the way, the word 'incompetent' has had a bad rap for far too long. The model helps us see that whenever we learn a new skill, not only is it okay to be incompetent, it is actually essential and a totally natural part of progress.

The four stages are:
1. **Unconscious incompetence:** The individual does not know what they do not know.
2. **Conscious incompetence**: Not only does the person not know what they do not know, they have so little ability that they demonstrate an almost helpless state.
3. **Conscious competence:** They now understand 'how to' but are not yet fully skilled.
4. **Unconscious competence:** The skill is now wired in so the individual can do it with little or no thought.

There is a fifth stage which is rarely discussed. We will look at this in Chapter 4.2.

Another way to look at these four stages is to see them as a process of moving off autopilot and eventually moving back onto autopilot once the new skill has been wired in. For example, I used to ski and decided to try out snowboarding. I was completely clueless (stage 1) as I thought it couldn't be too different from skiing. It really surprised me at just how different it was and even the most basic skills had to be relearned. Even using the snow tow (lift) with a snowboard felt completely different than with skis. Snowboarding highlighted how much I had relied on the skiing sticks, not just to help me turn but also for general balance. Interestingly, by going through the four stages of competence for the snowboard, it gave me a whole new perspective on skiing.

As you progress through this book, you will experience a number of competence shifts. For example, if you had never heard of delayed gratification before starting Part 0, you will have been in the state of unconscious incompetence (stage 1). After reading about it, you will already have moved up to stage 2 where you became consciously incompetent. Remember that incompetence is a vital phase of learning; being aware and acknowledging incompetence is the way out of delusion and denial, the two enemies of progress. Stages 3 and 4 depend on how you responded and continue to respond to the new information on delayed gratification. The fact that you are reading a book that takes an investment of your time shows that you are already on the path.

Chapter 0.5

Perceptual Filters

A while ago a TV show asked a group of students to take part in three wine tasting sessions. A different wine was tested at each session and the students were also asked to wear glasses with coloured lenses to test the effect the various colours had on their experience. The three wines were tested by the students as they wore blue, red and finally green lenses. In their feedback, the students agreed that the wine they'd tested while wearing the red-filtered glasses seemed to be sweeter than the other two. They looked totally bemused when it was revealed that all of the wines were identical. The experiment had been set up to demonstrate how colour affects our sense of taste. Perhaps the idea of rose-coloured glasses really do make things seem sweeter after all.

Perceptual filters are ways we look at things based on our expectations, assumptions, and experiences. We have already looked at delayed gratification which is a very useful perceptual filter. This is shown in Figure 3a below.

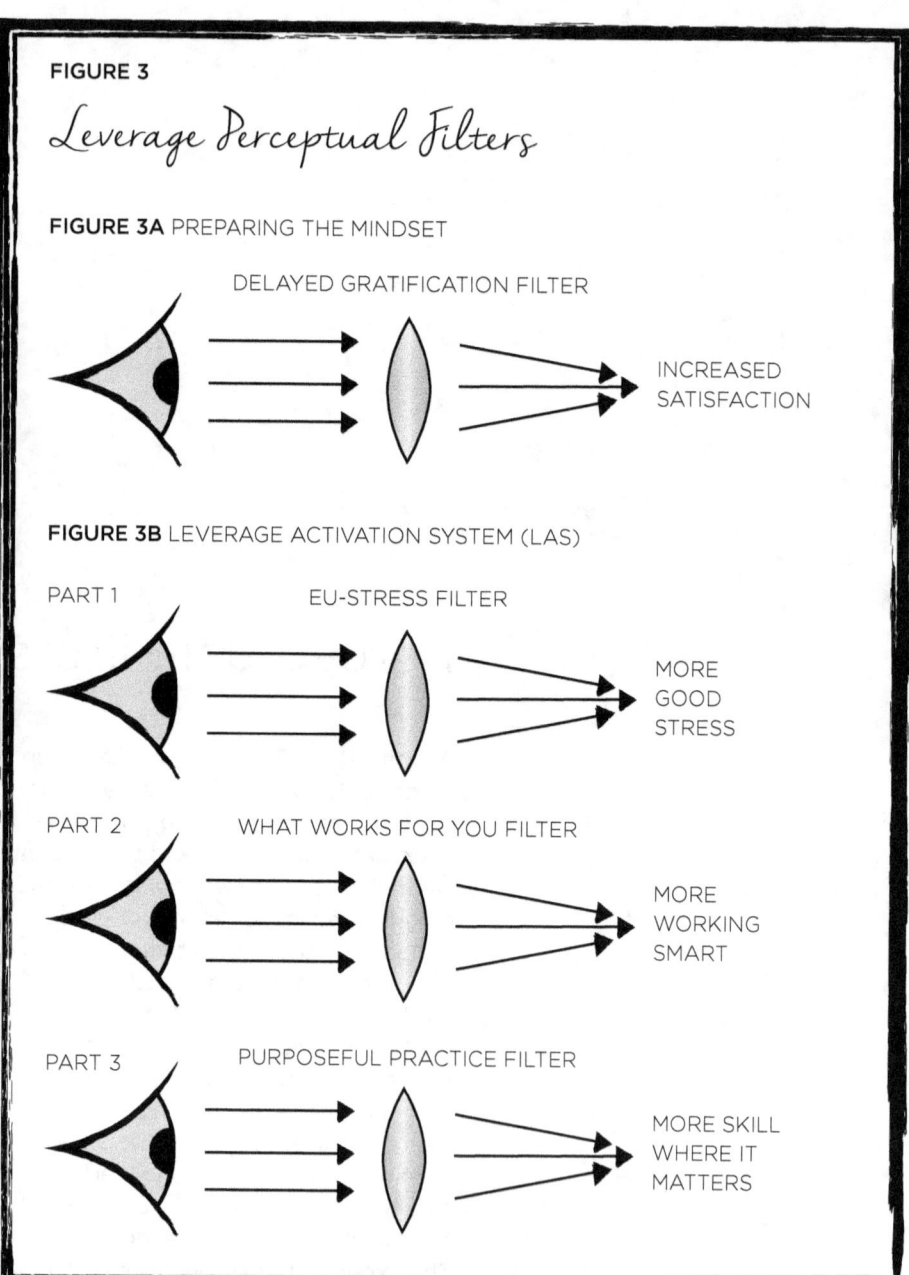

The delayed gratification filter could be compared to one of those pairs of coloured glasses that the students wore in their wine tasting sessions. When we open ourselves up to a possibility, it is very much like looking through a lens to test how that possibility would fit into our view of the world.

Here's an example of how you could test the delayed gratification filter for yourself. Some years back, a colleague told me how he'd wanted to buy a high-quality Swiss watch. He didn't want to go totally overboard with the purchase but at a cost of £1,500 to £2,000 for a used model, it was still quite a hefty investment. He agreed with his wife that he would save for the watch in the old-fashioned way. He'd save the pound coins that he'd normally spend on coffee on his way to work each morning. Every day he'd drop them into a glass jar, empty it into a bank account whenever it filled up and would only buy the watch when he had collected the full amount. When he bought the watch two years later, he felt both elated and grounded. It was the same feeling he'd experienced when he'd been rewarded for a good day's work. He told me that although he'd spent much more money on cars, there was no elation in these purchases. In fact he felt a bit let down, as though he'd cheated himself of that good feeling. He thought it was because there had not been the same delay and therefore there was no time to build anticipation.

Now let's look back at Figure 3b. You will see that three additional filters are shown. These will be covered as the book progresses. I just wanted to sow a seed in your mind visually for what is to come. We will make full use of your mind's ability to apply perceptual filters to test what could work for you to improve the quality of your life by applying leverage.

Chapter 0.6

Conscious And Subconscious Alignment

I assume that you already have some understanding of the differences between the conscious and subconscious mind. What we'll look at are the differences from the perspective of leverage. Figure 4 on the next page shows some differences that we'll find useful as we progress.

FIGURE 4

Conscious vs Subconscious Mind

SUBCONSCIOUS MIND	CONSCIOUS MIND
Processes an average of 40 million bits of information per second.[1]	Processes an average of 40 bits of information per second.[1]
Focused on keeping you safe.	Focused on what you desire.
Often described as the 'habitual mind'.	Often described as the 'volitional mind'.

[1] Tor Norretanders, *The User Illusion*

You may be surprised at how much more information is processed by the subconscious than the conscious mind. The million to one ratio is so huge that one can't help but see why it is that making life changes can be so tricky. This means that even though we may consciously focus on a desire the subconscious, which aims to keep you safe, will be the decision maker. And as the subconscious is what sustains our habits, the act of volition, i.e. making decisions, is somewhat limited. We always make decisions that are biased by our subconscious.

There are a number of ways to describe the divide between the conscious and subconscious. I like to visualise it as a set of scales with the fulcrum point being the intersection point at which crossover takes place in either direction. Hypnosis recognises that when the conscious desires and wants do not align with subconscious habits, we get to have problems, which are basically the conflict or gap between our desires and our habits. When a conflict or gap is resolved, this is commonly called a solution.

We all experience a range of external influences and factors which test us. Joseph Campbell's classic novel *Hero with a Thousand Faces* draws from world mythology to show us the archetypal hero's journey. George Lucas drew from this book when he created Luke Skywalker and *Star Wars*. The hero's triumph over challenges suggests that a problem-free life is maybe not what life is meant to be and nor is it the secret to happiness as many believe. Instead, it is about learning effectively from life as we experience problems but do not dwell on them. The problems are a way to propel us forward so they can be thought of as a springboard to a better life where we tap into more of our potential.

Developing character through life's challenges is so important to us that if you look at Oscar winning films over the years, you will see that the hero's journey is usually the backdrop to the movie. *Gladiator, Slumdog Millionaire, The King's Speech* were all typical in that each showed people facing adversity and winning against all the odds.

As we move forward, we will look at how we can learn to consciously interact with the subconscious mind via language patterns and energetics. The more we tap into its nature, the more we will narrow the gap between our conscious wants and subconscious habits.

We have already discussed delayed gratification and the important role that trust plays when we begin to develop it. Trust is just one of the dynamics that the subconscious recognises so this gives us another way to connect with it. As we progress, we will tap into how we can use ideas from hypnosis to recognise the gap between the conscious and subconscious so we can experience the growth that problems bring us while getting to the solutions faster.

Chapter 0.7

The Spring Clean Effect

In November 2014 I finished a four-year contract and decided to take a break from working to complete the outline for this book. I'd mentioned this in a conversation with a group of friends and Andy, a well-respected friend and entrepreneur from the USA, invited me to go and stay with him and his family out in California while I did it. I can't recall his exact words as the Beach Boys were already playing in the background of my mind.

As I turned to another friend just to make sure I hadn't misheard the incredible invitation, my other friend said: "There are opportunities that pop up in life and you don't win points with the universe by not taking them." So the decision was made and the next challenge was what to do with my property during that time. It was as if the gods were listening. A few days later, a Kung Fu buddy told me his new mortgage application had been delayed and he needed a place for him, his girlfriend and two cats to stay. The solution was at hand. The universe must have been bringing the planets into alignment for us.

I got a secondary gain when I decided to clear out my home before I went away and my new lodgers moved in. It was my first big clear-out in around seven years.

Two things jumped out at me. The first was just how much stuff I had gathered as it took so much effort to clear things out. I had to create three distinct areas in one room; one pile was to keep, one was for recycling and the other was for those things I wasn't sure about. The 'not sure' pile took a lot more time than the other two and eventually I started asking myself 'have I used this in the last year?' If I hadn't, it went straight to the charity shop or to recycling because I clearly didn't need it and was only holding onto it out of habit.

The second thing that jumped out at me was how much lighter I felt after the clean-out. It was the same feeling I'd had in my early thirties when I took a sabbatical to travel the world. Everything I needed fitted into one backpack. Life felt very simple indeed.

I had left it way too long since my last major clean-out and I vowed not to let things build up like that again. Later on we will look at how to ensure we don't let unwanted things clutter up our lives. Decluttering is energising and frees up more energy - it even works with our personal computers. If we let too much information build up on them, performance can be affected. Therefore we need to be mindful of the effect of capacity on effectiveness. More is not necessarily best.

Recapitulation of Terms

Learning - Growing and connecting neural networks.

Delayed Gratification - The measure of increased satisfaction that comes from resisting a smaller but more immediate reward in order to receive a larger or more enduring reward later.

Perceptual filter - The way we look at things based on expectations, assumptions, experiences we've had and also new ideas.

Reticular Activation System (RAS) - Part of the brain responsible for supplying integrated filtered responses to outside stimuli via a way of deleting, distorting and generalising. It is our noticing faculty.

> I love those who can smile in trouble, who can gather strength from distress, and grow brave by reflection.

LEONARDO DA VINCI

Part 1

The Eustress Filter (Initiating Leverage)

> "No idea is so outlandish that it should not be considered with a searching but at the same time a steady eye."
>
> WINSTON CHURCHILL

> Great minds discuss ideas; average minds discuss events; small minds discuss people.

ELEANOR ROOSEVELT

Aim To help you see how even the simplest idea can make for a substantial change.

Concepts
1 Ideo Dynamics
2 Yerkes-Dodson Law
3 Distress vs. Eustress

Chapter 1.1

Ideo Dynamic Leverage

'Ideo dynamic' is another way of saying 'by the power of an idea' and the term comes from the field of hypnosis. The complex and intangible nature of the mind means that hypnosis can't be ranked as one of the sciences but that is no reason to overlook it. Hypnosis faces one of the most difficult challenges - mediating between the conscious and subconscious. These two are like oil and water: it is as though the conscious mind wants to speak the Queen's English while the subconscious would rather use images, symbols and sign language.

I use ideas from hypnosis throughout this book because for me it is the fulcrum point between the conscious and subconscious. Its ideas help the other ideas and concepts in this book come together naturally.

Dr Kelly McGonigal, health psychologist and author of *The Willpower Instinct*, gave an informative and inspirational TED talk in 2013 called 'How to make stress your friend'. Kelly shared a number of scientific findings about stress including one from a study that had been conducted by Harvard University. The study comprised two groups of people. One control group was told about how bad stress was for them. The other group was told how the sensations of stress were really there to help the body achieve maximum performance so stress was actually energising and a good thing. Both groups then took part in a stressful environment test.

When non-invasive tests were done on the hearts of the two groups, it was discovered that constrictions of blood vessels were evident in the group who believed stress was bad for them. Restricted blood vessels are a common factor in the lead up to cardiovascular disease.

The second group showed no blood vessel constriction. Their bodies showed physiological signs associated with having experienced joy and courage. So even though their hearts pounded just as much as those in the first group, their hearts showed a relaxed vascular profile.

Here a new idea became a perceptual filter - stress can be good - and it allowed the people in the second group to experience a tangible physiological and mental shift.

The Yerkes-Dodson Law

Devised by psychologists Robert M. Yerkes and John Dodson in 1908, the Yerkes–Dodson law is a useful model that provides a relationship between arousal and performance, especially in the study of maximising performance.

As Figure 5 on the next page shows, the curve gives a visual representation of how arousal can help us perform better - but only up to a limit. Of course, the types of activities will vary as will the mental state of the person experiencing the arousal.

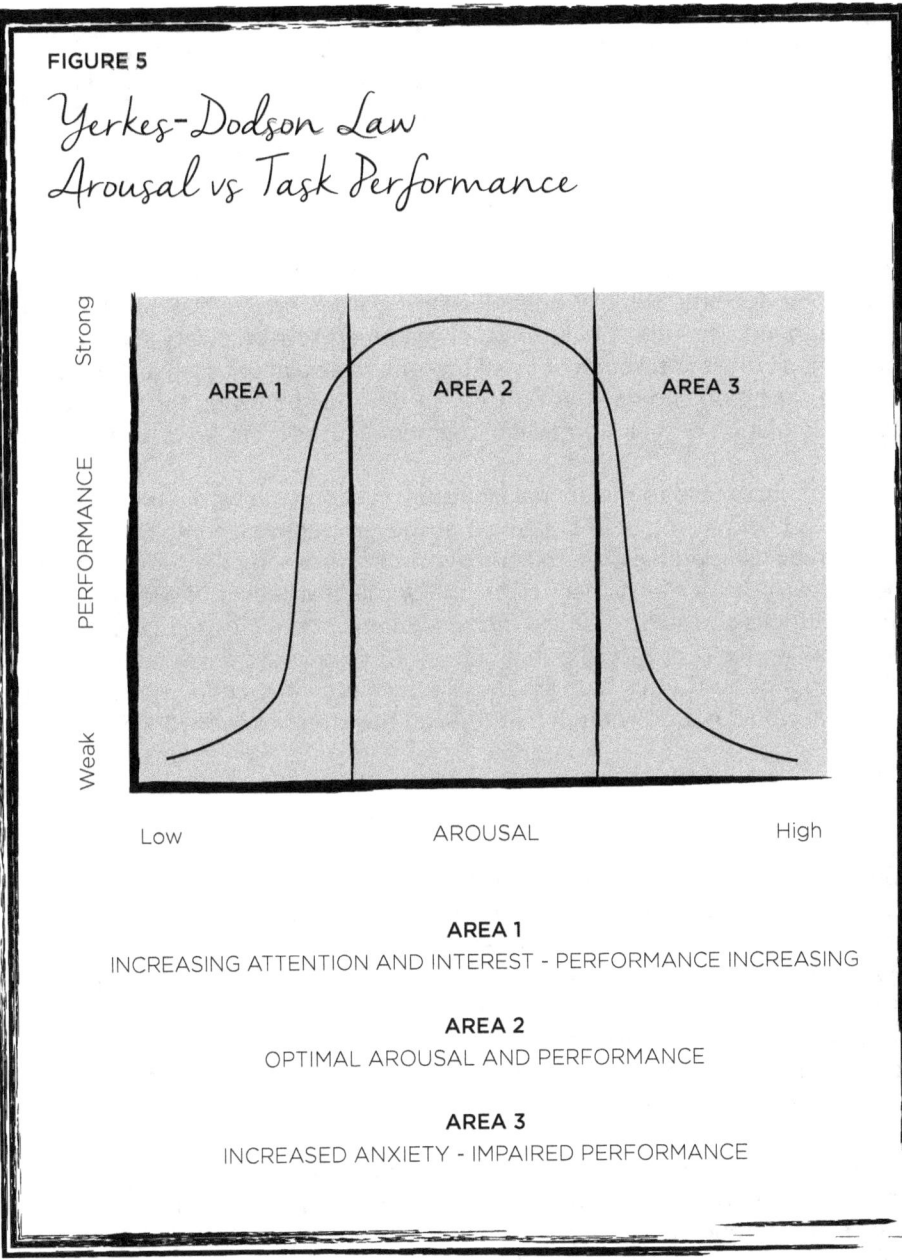

The Yerkes-Dodson model helps us understand:

1. That the nervous system can be compared to an elastic band. When it is slack, it doesn't do what it is meant to do. When stretched too tight, it loses elasticity. The zone in the middle of these two extremes is the healthy elastic zone.

2. Why breaking skill development into smaller or larger skill sets can help people learn better. When someone begins to master a new skill, if it is not sized well in terms of the amount of arousal required to perform, it will either feel too simple or too difficult. If the skill is sized such that it fits into the middle zone, this allows for optimal performance and learning can feel more natural. This middle zone is the best position for learning.

This performance/arousal graph shows that we tend to work well within a certain zone. Too little stimulation and we get bored; too much stimulation and we get fatigued. The rule applies to other mammals too. Wild cats in captivity show signs of distress through unusual repetitive behaviours such as turning in circles or pacing up and down for hours at a time. Withdrawing them from the natural stimulation of their normal environment causes them great stress.

It's not just applicable to the animal kingdom. In Japan the work ethic has in some areas become so out of balance that they even have a name for it. Karoshi, which can be translated as 'death from overwork', is exactly that - occupational sudden death. There's a link here to the major medical causes of death such as heart attacks and stroke, far too many of them caused by stress. In some areas, working for 12 or more hours a day, six or seven days a week, year after year is commonplace. This is an area where even the intervention shared by Dr McGonigal would not be enough to outweigh the effect of overwork.

Eustress/Distress Zones

Sports psychology splits stress into eustress (good stress) and distress (bad stress). If we look back to Figure 5, we see how the eustress/distress idea aligns with the Yerkes-Dodson curve. For example, for an athlete to achieve peak they have to constantly push their limits while avoiding injury. If the athlete operates in Area 1 of the graph, they will underperform and not reach their true potential. If they work in Area 3, they'll be at risk of overtraining, exhaustion and injury. Area 2 is where the athlete stretches their ability but also ensures they balance performance with enough rest, nutrition and preparation work.

In recent years a lot of sportspeople have moved from amateur to professional status. This is partly because they know that achieving very high levels of performance through part-time training is near impossible. By making sport their profession, they are able to balance their training adequately and build enough rest into their schedule, because they know that rest is an absolutely crucial component of high level performance.

No matter what sort of job you have, everyone needs to work as much as possible within their eustress zone. The work itself is important but it must be balanced by sufficient rest whether that comes in the form of regular breaks, practicing meditation or even power naps.

Natural Timing...

The Daoist Water Method places huge emphasis on people opening or unfolding in their own time. Sometimes we see something like this in the Western world where some children don't do well at school but find their niche later on in life.

Unlike other Western countries, Scandinavia puts less emphasis on children moving into the formal education environment too soon, and this philosophy is paying off. In 2012, Business Insider published a global league table (from the Economist Intelligence Unit) which showed that Finland had the best education system in the world. The study had gathered and processed international test results and data such as graduation rates between 2006 and 2010.

For Finland, this was no fluke as they had implemented huge educational reforms some 40 years earlier. They simply went back to basics and ditched the evaluation-driven, centralised model that much of the Western world uses. They adopted the pedagogy mindset where the child's natural development was the key factor. Pedagogy (from Greek paidagōgia, 'to lead a child') is the discipline that deals with the theory and practice of education; it concerns the study and practice of how to bring out the best of the individual through teaching.

This book aims to follow a similar route with the Water Method which will help you gently find your eustress zone so you can stretch yourself wisely whenever you need to meet life's challenges. Yet you will be able to gauge where you have crossed over into distress so you can then get more skilled at seeing what works for you and what doesn't work for you. The Water Method will guide you towards eustress which is an indicator that you are experiencing more of what works for you as an individual, more of the time.

EXPERIENCE 2: ELASTIC ZONE EXERCISE

Look back at Figure 5. Now take a medium-sized elastic band. Hold the band between your right hand and left hand. Start with the elastic totally slack then gently stretch the band until it gets to a point where you can feel the elastic starting to stretch.

Stop. This is equivalent to the starting point of the Eustress zone.

Then stretch further until the elastic starts to feel taut.

Stop. This is equivalent to the stopping point of the Eustress zone.

This Daoist idea uses a prop to help us understand a concept both physically and mentally.

This experience helps us define the boundaries of the Eustress Zone which is Area 2 in Figure 5.

Throughout this book, we will look at many ideo dynamics (power of ideas) to help steer your life into the good stress zone while adding extra leverage so that you can work on improving the overall quality of your life.

> ### Summary
>
> - Stress can be good for us and changing how we look at it can affect us even at a physiological level.
>
> - Separating stress into good stress (eustress) and bad stress (distress) and working in the middle zone helps us get the most from our efforts and energies.
>
> - By applying the Daoist Water Method we get better at finding out what works for us, especially our own natural timing.

In the next chapter we look at the power of a simple pause which will be useful later when we learn about a de-hypnosis technique called defractionation.

> "The right word may be effective, but no word was ever as effective as a rightly timed pause."
>
> MARK TWAIN

Aim To raise awareness of an idea that shows us how we can tap into our natural timing.

Concepts
1. Vacation Effect
2. Alpha Sandwich
3. Power Naps

By The Power Of A Pause

In this chapter we'll add the power of a pause to the power of an idea (ideo-dynamic); you could also call it the vacation effect and you may have experienced it yourself.

In a memorable episode of a home transformation TV show, a guy who'd embarked on a huge home expansion project was really struggling. The presenter met him at the halfway stage and said she thought he was going to miss his deadline. The deadline was important as overrunning would have bad financial consequences for his family. Then he hesitantly told the presenter that he and his wife and child were taking a two-week vacation. The presenter was concerned - surely he'd fall even further behind on his schedule? But he insisted it was the right thing to do.

The presenter returned a few months later and to her complete surprise, he had made the deadline. She was bemused about how he had done it. He explained that on her last visit he had felt so tired and worn out that he'd seemed to be going around in circles and getting in his own way with everything he attempted. It had been one step forward, three steps back. However, when he returned from two weeks' rest in the sunshine, it was as if his mind had resolved all his tasks and priorities on its own and the building and decoration work just flowed from that point on. Everything fell into place. He also felt physically refreshed and actually looked forward to the hard work that was ahead of him whereas before the holiday he had dreaded it.

Once we get to a certain level of fatigue, we tend to get in our own way. But just as this guy showed, when the subconscious is given some space, it can do a lot of the work for us. At times like this, our job is to consciously take a break.

When we have too much distress and not enough eustress in our lives, it's impossible to see simple solutions. We have to give our mind a break. As the Bible teaches, we need to rest at least one day in seven. Farmers know that even the land needs a rest from time to time and that's why they use crop rotation so the land can rest and renew itself every seven years.

Have you ever tried remembering something when you're stressed out (i.e. in a state of distress)? It's as though we're pushing the answer away. Yet later, when we've stopped trying and when we're thinking of something completely different, the answer will just pop into our minds.

Competitors on TV quizzes endure a more extreme version - they'd easily answer the questions if they were relaxing at home (eustress) but now they're sweating under the lights in a TV studio (distress) the answers elude them. Of course, some people thrive on situational pressure and their performance improves. Their eustress zone is such that pressure like this allows them to harness their focus and attention.

Science Supports Pausing

A study from Columbia University found that we can make more than 70 decisions a day ranging from simple ones, such as what to eat for breakfast, to more important and complex ones. Our brains need to rest just as much as our muscles do and people often 'sleep on it' before reaching an important decision. I follow that advice myself as it has proven effective and I want to make good choices because the decisions we make today always stay with us.

We're less effective at making decisions when we're fatigued. Columbia University Medical Center (CUMC) researchers discovered that if you postpone making a decision for just a fraction of a second, you actually improve the accuracy of that decision. This allows your brain to focus on the actual decision being made and block out distractions.

Although I've yet to find studies to fully support this, my intuition is that when we pause we create an 'Alpha Sandwich'. Let me explain what I mean. As you are reading these words, your brain is producing beta waves (in the region of 13-30 Hz). A predominance of beta waves is associated with being alert and active, your brain's in beta whenever you concentrate on learning something or doing an activity that requires focus. So you need your brain to generate beta waves in order to think and function consciously.

When you want to relax or chill out, it's time to shift into alpha (in the region of 8 - 13 Hz). Alpha is the brainwave associated with relaxed and daydreaming states of mind; it's relaxed, detached awareness. If you're like most people, when you close your eyes and take a few slow, deep breaths you'll experience a light, relaxed alpha state. Some consider alpha the gateway to meditation. Others think alpha waves are the link between the conscious and the subconscious mind.

It's possible that when we pause, we shift from beta into alpha and then back to beta, i.e. an alpha sandwich. When we pause, we gain access to the best of beta and alpha states and this helps us make a better decision.

Neuroscientist Jonah Lehrer, author of *How We Decide*, points out that people who experience damage to the emotional centres of their brain are unable to make decisions. He argues that there is a sweet spot between logic and emotion that makes for good decisions. I think this supports my intuition that when we pause to make a decision, we are more in balance. The pause is a kind of pivot point between thinking and feeling.

Later in Part 2, we will look at how to use the pausing pivot point in a very practical sense.

The Power Of Power Naps

Power naps, briefly mentioned in Chapter 1.1, are one way to experience the eustress zone more often in our busy daily lives. The book *Take a Nap! Change Your Life* by Sara Mednick PhD expands on this idea.

There is currently a fatigue epidemic afflicting millions of people all over the world. Sara, a researcher at the Salk Institute and the leading authority on the study of napping, provides a scientifically-based breakthrough programme that shows how we can fight fatigue through a custom-designed nap. There are many advantages to napping, including increased alertness, creativity boosts and improved powers of perception. The trick behind effective power naps is simple: the right nap at the right time.

Sara's study of the five phases of sleep has helped her advise others on how to set up a personal sleep profile and schedule power naps at optimum times. The study is so well formulated that it is possible to design a nap to inspire creativity one day and memory the next day.

After her visits to Google's headquarters, they and other leading edge companies began to support and encourage power naps. They saw the potential because their company particularly values innovation and creativity.

This pausing effect will be discussed much more in Part 2 through a concept called defractionation.

Summary

- The vacation effect shows us that when we have a fresh mind, we don't get in our own way so much.

- Science proves that pauses lead to better decisions.

- Scientific studies show that good decisions come from a balanced place between logic and emotion.

The mind is impressed by proof. In the next chapter we'll look at how we can use that fact to guide ourselves into the eustress zone.

> The measure of who we are is what we do with what we have.
>
> VINCE LOMBARDI

Aim To begin activating the RAS to automatically search out and bring more eustress into our daily lives.

Concepts
1 SUD
2 SUE

Chapter 1.3

What You Can Measure You Can Improve

Whenever we make a change we measure its results whether that's done consciously or unconsciously. We need a reliable cause and effect relationship so that we can trust the measurement to give us accurate feedback. Trust plays as important a role in change as it did for the children in the Stanford marshmallow experiment.

Measuring change and/or improvement can be as simple as marking a child's height on the wall. Did you ever do that? It was great seeing how I'd grown every time we did this at home. However, like so many useful things we tend to take measurement and the tools that do it for granted. Yet clocks didn't always exist, nor did slide rules or compasses.

The Marine Chronometer

Early explorers made use of the stars and sun position in navigation and it served them well for millennia. Their kind of navigation was more about successive approximation where a typical journey would likely be more than three times the point to point distance because of the continuous error correction that eventually got them to their final destination.

Latitude measurement was reliable, however longitude (East-West position) was such a problem that, following the Scilly naval disaster of 1707, the British Government offered the Longitude prize of £20,000 (£2.75m today). There was fierce competition for the prize. The challenge was to design a timepiece that worked accurately and repeatedly despite extreme variations in movement, temperature, vibration and salty air environment.

John Harrison, a self-educated English carpenter and clockmaker, invented the marine chronometer and took the prize. This first ever 'sea clock' was revolutionary. Pivotal points in human evolution have been linked to measurement inventions. The pendulum and atomic clocks are other examples of inventions that have led to shifts in the way we live. Time and how it is measured has a massive effect on us, perhaps because we use dates and times to pinpoint life's important moments and use time to bring order to our experiences. Yet time is a subjective matter. A mile is always a mile, but an hour can feel like a moment.

> When you are courting a nice girl, an hour seems like a second. When you sit on a red-hot cinder for a second, it seems like an hour. That's relativity.
>
> ALBERT EINSTEIN

A problem mindset and a solution mindset are only separated by the length of time we experience what we don't want to experience. Problems are a part of life. The better we get at measuring the relative time that we experience problems, the faster we can learn from them and move on. A person with a solution mindset has the same experiences as us, but with just one difference... they have the skills to learn swiftly so problems rarely last longer than necessary.

Subjective Units Of Distress Scale (SUDS)

The Subjective Units of Distress Scale (SUDS) runs from 0 to 10 and measures the subjective intensity of disturbance or distress currently being experienced by an individual. The individual self-assesses where they are on the scale. The SUDS may be used as a benchmark for someone to evaluate the progress of a medical treatment or any change in life.

The SUDS is linked back to 1969 and the work of Joseph Wolpe, a South African psychiatrist, who used it in cognitive-behavioural treatments and for research purposes. It's called subjective because the person decides where they are on the scale.

It's simple to use, as simple as asking: "On a scale of 0 to 10, where one is the best you can feel and 10 is the worst, how do you feel right now?" Ask this question over a period of time (and record your answers) and there you have it, an easy way to gauge changes, hopefully improvements.

Subjective Units Of Eustress Scale (SUES)

Although we have a SUD Scale for measuring disturbance or distress, we don't have a similar tool to measure eustress. This may not surprise you, but it certainly surprised me. Could this reveal that we are very skilled at measuring and evaluating pain and suffering but less skilled at measuring well-being and happiness? What we choose to measure says a lot about our perceptual filters and unconscious view of the world.

Working With Resistance

That missing measurement scale for eustress is a great example of the mind's tricky and elusive nature. When we believe something has the potential to bring change, the threat of change can bring up a ton of resistance from the subconscious mind as its role is to keep you safe, not necessarily happy. Resistance to change is completely normal even though we may feel uncomfortable about acknowledging that. Do you recall Figure 4 which showed the huge difference between the bits per second processed by the conscious and subconscious minds? The ratio is one million to one in favour of the subconscious. That means that our volition (exercise of willing) is completely outweighed by existing habits.

Even when we intuit that something would be better for us, we can find that the anchor of the past is so substantial that denial is less painful, at least in the short term. We might then be drawn towards some form of immediate gratification as a temporary relief so that we don't even have to think about the change that could benefit us in the long term.

On a positive note, the mind is willing to examine new evidence. You wouldn't be reading this otherwise. This can be compared to how science works through various stages from the conception of an idea to the point where it may be widely accepted by the scientific community. It incrementally gathers evidence that gains support until a momentum is formed that carries it over the line of being accepted as 'truth'.

Tapping Into Your RAS

In Part 0 we looked at perceptual filters and how we delete, distort and generalise. This is an automated system that is continually updated by what we focus on in our everyday life. As you read this, you might wonder how we update something that's automatic, especially if it's the very same system that directs what impressions we allow into our consciousness. Well that is worth wondering about.

There are a number of ways to tap into this automatic ability, in fact we've already started with introducing a number of ideo dynamics. Other ways include:

- Applying our awareness (as we picked up from the double slit experiment).
- Knowing about distress and eustress and so being able to see the difference between good/constructive changes and bad/not constructive changes.

So how can we apply these three ideas to tap into our RAS?

Most things in life have an upside and a downside. There's usually an element of distress and an element of eustress in all of our daily activities. The following experience demonstrates this so please do it now before you read on.

Note: if you feel any resistance to doing this exercise, you are actually on the right track.

EXPERIENCE 3: EUSTRESS VERSUS DISTRESS

Instructions
1. Fill out the blank second table with a list of things that you usually do.
2. Now decide on the right percentage for eustress and distress; e.g. shopping could be 90% eustress or 90% distress depending on your own feelings about it!
3. The first table is just an example to get you started.
4. Please note that blank tables can be downloaded from http://www.findingthefulcrum.org.

Table 1: *Kieran O'Connor* (name)

	ACTIVITY	EUSTRESS %	DISTRESS %	TOTAL %
1.	Watching a great movie at the cinema	100	0	100
2.	Grocery shopping	80	20	100
3.	Catching up on social media	85	15	100
4.	Commuting	90	10	100
5.	Watching sports on TV	95	5	100
6.	Dental appointments	70	30	100
7.	Beers with buddies	100	0	100
8.	Completing my financial accounts	10	90	100
9.	Practicing Kung Fu	95	5	100
10.	Writing this book	90	10	100

Table 2: _____ (name)

	ACTIVITY	EUSTRESS %	DISTRESS %	TOTAL %
1.				100
2.				100
3.				100
4.				100
5.				100
6.				100
7.				100
8.				100
9.				100
10.				100

Okay, so you have completed the blank sheet, haven't you? If your distress level is still too high to introduce this new experience at this stage of the book, add a single line item activity as 'Completing Experience 3' and for now just add your current level of eustress and distress.

You can always come back and complete this experience later in full with more enjoyment as your overall distress level reduces and eustress level increases. The chances are that you'll learn a lot from the eustress/distress split. Not wanting to complete the experience will help you gain an insight into the resistance that was offered by your subconscious mind. The eustress/distress split itself is so simple to apply yet so effective that its efficacy can be very easily dismissed.

Another way to describe the distress/eustress split is 'divide and conquer'. Splitting stress up into two parts is great for freeing us from the bonds of things that used to stress us in the past. Just because they used to cause us stress doesn't mean that they'll continue to give us distress.

Experience 3 could just be completed mentally and that will still bring some benefit. However the pen to paper aspect is very powerful as documenting our thoughts provides data and evidence that our subconscious cannot easily dismiss.

As we write, we are also reading what we are writing which of course is obvious. I won't go into detail here but this means that a very influential feedback loop is created at the subconscious level. It is as if ideas make more sense to us when they are converted from thinking to writing whether that is in the form of words, diagrams or pictures. This explains why I completed my very first outline structure for this book (which was a brainstorming process) with pen and paper. I followed a system called Mind Mapping which I can highly recommend researching if you have never experienced it.

In addition, writing uses our physiology much more than thinking does. If you do a web search on how many muscles are involved in something as simple as putting pen to paper, you might be amazed. This does however help explain why the world of robotics is finding the physical art of writing such a challenge to replicate.

In essence, pen to paper provides leverage in many ways so if you want to tap into your subconscious more effectively, play with this thought... 'If you want to make life better, write it in a letter'. Of course, you might say that a letter is something that you send to someone. Well that someone is your subconscious mind whenever you write something down.

Change itself will depend on many factors, including:
   a. How willing we are to be truthful with ourselves and write that truth on paper.
   b. How willing we are to repeat this exercise.
   c. How willing we are to be gracious to our subconscious when it uses our RAS faculty to take us into the eustress zone more often. A sincere 'thank you' can go a long way!

Willingness is important so the conscious mind does have its part to play in making change. It is just that we are now allowing the conscious mind to become more aligned with the subconscious by talking a language that both can understand.

Time Flies When...

Most of us know what it is like to be so absorbed in something that you lose track of all time. I was like that when I first saw *Star Wars* as a kid. On the other hand, we also know what it feels like when the second hand on our watch seems to be going backwards. I recall working the days between Christmas Day and New Year once. Those days felt so long and drawn out that I vowed I'd never do it again.

Time plays a big part in how we experience our lives. When I was researching this chapter I wondered if the pace of life had picked up so much in the last few years that we have lost touch with our own personal timing. It's useful for us to be mindful about how 'living by the clock' can lead to distress. Disengaging from that stopwatch mentality and making more use of our awareness and senses will lead us into eustress more often... more naturally.

Summary

- There is a measurement system for distress called Suggestive Units of Distress (SUD).

- We have introduced a new measure called Suggestive Units of Eustress (SUE).

- Time gives us a direct relationship with SUD and SUE. Generally speaking SUE helps time pass faster.

Recapitulation of Terms

Distress - The aspect of stress that we associate negatively with mental, emotional and physical strain.

Eustress - The positive aspect of stress where we stretch within a zone that brings out the best in us mentally, emotionally and physically.

SUD - Suggestive Units of Distress. A scale of 0 to 10 that indicates an individual's level of distress.

SUE - Suggestive Units of Eustress. A scale of 0 to 10 that indicates an individual's level of eustress.

In the next chapter we will look at the elusions and illusions that anchor us in distress.

> Motivation is what gets you started. Habit is what keeps you going.

JIM ROHN

Part 2

The What Works Filter (Transitional Leverage)

> "Reality is merely an illusion, albeit a very persistent one."
>
> ALBERT EINSTEIN

> We are drowning in information but starved for knowledge.

JOHN NAISBITT

Aim To strip back the 'problem' so we have more clarity before we start seeking the 'solution'.

Concepts
1 The Illusion of a Mistake.

2 The Simplicity Paradox.

3 The Zeigarnik Effect.

The Elaborate Elusions

Let's kick off by following John Naisbitt's advice and define the words that make up this chapter's title.

Elaborate: (From Dictionary.com)
- Worked out with care and nicety of detail; executed with great minuteness.

- Marked by intricate and often excessive detail; complicated; ornate.

Elusion:
- The act of eluding; evasion.

Elaborate has a two-sided nature as it can be both exquisitely detailed and/or needlessly complicated; it can work for or against us.

Elusion is another word for evasion, which has negative connotations although elusiveness can sometimes be a useful skill.

It's a useful word for us too, partly because of that fundamental concept the 'elusive obvious', and also because using words that aren't in our usual vocabulary wakes us up a little. It can subtly help us in the precarious task of turning a spotlight on our blind spots and our habitual nature. Its evasiveness helps us see that it's as if the RAS plays tricks on us. As we work through this chapter, elusion will gradually be replaced by...

Illusion: (From Dictionary.com)
- Something that deceives by producing a false or misleading impression of reality.
- *Psychology.* A perception, as of visual stimuli (optical illusion) that represents what is perceived in a different way from the way it is in reality.

The aim here is to incrementally start testing what is almost too obvious to see due to our habitual nature. What we also want to do is enjoy the process as much as possible.

I love watching magic tricks; they bring out the excitable kid in me. Whenever stage magicians reveal their methods, whether that's by mistake or by design, there can be a sense of disappointment because so often the illusion is almost too simple. American illusionists Penn and Teller use this to great effect at times. They perform a complex trick for the audience and then reveal how they did it, which the audience usually enjoys but there's also a sense of 'is that it?' Then to top things off, they repeat the trick but in such a way that the illusion they'd used before cannot be used again. It's like they have a magical contingency plan. This is where the audience experiences the wow effect.

We will look at three of many elusive areas in life that we so easily buy into, perhaps just because of human nature where we occasionally achieve brief moments of clarity in a world of confusion...or so we like to believe.

These are the three illusions that have most relevance when we're talking about leverage:

1. We underestimate the need for closure.
2. When we look back, we think we could have somehow done better.
3. We believe that trying harder is the solution.

1. We Underestimate The Need For Closure.

Moore's Law (named after Intel co-founder Gordon Moore) observed in 1965 that transistors were shrinking so fast that every year twice as many could fit onto a chip. In 1975 the pace picked up even more so the rate doubled every two years.

Moore's Law is still true today. We are now living with the effects of the exponential growth in the power of computer chips over the past five decades.

The average person now has a mobile phone that's more powerful than the computer that first got man to land on the moon. We live in a society where speed, convenience and throwing things away is worshipped; a society where wisdom is pushed into the background.

Please understand that I am not knocking the technology we have today. I love gadgets. It is just that we seem to be working harder than ever while the freedom we desire is being held out to us like a carrot in front of a donkey. Just like the donkey, we never quite get it.

> ...as a model of a complex system becomes more complete, it becomes less understandable. So, why do we seek complexity?

The paradox of simplicity helps us see that as a model of a complex system becomes more complete, it becomes less understandable. So, why do we seek complexity?

I believe that we have confused two separate things.

The Zeigarnik Effect, named after Russian psychologist Bluma Zeigarnik, came about after she made an observation whilst in a restaurant in Vienna. The waiters managed many orders both on paper and in their heads, yet they seemed to make a deal with their minds in that they would remember the orders very well, but, when the orders were completed, they would almost instantly evaporate from their memory. If asked about an order that had been completed say half an hour earlier, it was as if it had never happened.

There is an interesting follow up to this. Restaurants have found that when food is sent back for any reason, it only takes a few to destabilise the smooth running of the restaurant. It is not just the kitchen that gets thrown out of sequence; the waiting staff can be thrown out of sync too.

Zeigarnik tested her ideas in lab conditions with simple tasks and puzzles being completed by groups of people. The groups were split so some tasks were allowed to be completed and some were interrupted. Recollection of incomplete tasks proved to be much higher than completed ones.

I remember going to a bar in Dublin with some colleagues one night. It looked just like your average pub until I noticed that there was only one barman and the customers were two deep all along the bar. I thought it'd take hours to buy my round but when I observed this man, he was like a circus act. He was taking orders, serving drinks and taking money from about six people at any time. His skills were amazing and even his pouring of multiple pints of Guinness was right on the mark, which is difficult for most bar staff even if they're pouring one at a time.

I was served miraculously fast and I couldn't help but emphasise how impressed I was. One of my colleagues said the barman was well-known locally because he'd gone through a structured apprenticeship and was considered a master of his trade. He'd been taught the skills step by step in a very different manner to many parts of the world where a bar job is considered a stepping stone to a 'proper job'. A well-trained barperson is held in high esteem in Dublin and a huge part of their professionalism is being able to multitask effectively, i.e. the ability to let go of completed tasks and hold in mind the multiple tasks that have not been completed yet.

The Zeigarnik Effect tells us that our memory is able to recall incomplete or interrupted tasks far better than completed ones.

Of course, everything has a context so there are other factors to consider. It seems that remembrance is a science in itself. Further research on remembrance showed that we are able to compartmentalise life and memories somehow. Although we could split memory into short, medium and long term, I would like to look a bit more at the two ends of the spectrum, the short and long term, which Zeigarnik's findings helped me understand:

Open Loops
The human mind is quite incredible in how much data it can handle. What we know is that boredom and feeling overwhelmed form two ends of a spectrum. They could also be called understimulation or overstimulation. Both extremes create distress. Somewhere in between, we find eustress where having a number of open loops feels good for us. This is where we feel enthusiastic and successful. What we also find is that periods of understimulation (such as a relaxing vacation) and overstimulation (such as a critical deadline) work well as long as the ratios of time we spend in each zone all balance out.

Open Loops In TV And Movies
The first *Matrix* film had a big impact on me. Rather than leaving during the credits as usual, I sat right to the end trying to make as much sense as possible of the messages contained within the movie. I quite enjoyed the second of the three movies due to the amazing action scenes but was hugely disappointed in the third one. The *Matrix* didn't work as a trilogy for me, unlike *The Lord of the Rings*. It was written as a trilogy and all three movies linked together naturally. Successful loops are not easy to create in movies if they're not done right from the outset.

We've always had an insatiable appetite for great novels, TV series and movie sagas. I remember someone telling me about how as a young boy he'd run with excitement to the local cinema each Saturday morning to see the latest Flash Gordon adventure.

Next time you're catching up with your favourite TV show or film, why not look out for the ways the entertainment experts hook you with open loops so that you will tune in again. This might give you an insight into where your own habits hook you.

Resolution (Re-Solution)

Resolution could also be described as completion, closure and even making amends. It's an important idea as it is relevant to our mental, emotional, physical and spiritual health.

Although not wanting to go too deep here, it's useful to consider that there is a natural cycle to all feelings, emotions and sensations and it is when this cycle is interrupted that problems usually come up. We have been led to believe, for example, that grief is only related to extreme events like the loss of a loved one.

Elisabeth Kübler-Ross, a Swiss-American psychiatrist, was a pioneer in near-death studies and the author of the groundbreaking book *On Death and Dying* (1969), where she first discussed her theory of the five stages of grief. This theory talks about the grieving process and has greatly helped people who were stuck in grief. The five stages are: denial, anger, bargaining, depression and acceptance. Although grief and loss is a subjective experience, it helps people enormously if they know that they are working through a natural process and that what they are experiencing is totally understandable and even logical. But it is not just bereavement that can cause us grief and feelings of loss. The loss of just about anything can pass through those five stages. The loss of a job, a divorce (especially for the children), and all the way through to the loss of physical things such as having something stolen from us, all can feel very similar to a bereavement.

And when we decide to change our lives, we lose the old way of doing things; whenever we make a change, there is always a price to pay. Even if the change is potentially hugely beneficial, the subconscious can still bring up resistance as it knows that there will be a degree of grief and loss associated with making that change.

It is not just grief that needs closure; other painful emotions need it too. From time to time in martial arts we have to train as close to a real-life violent encounter as possible so we don't have to think too much should a real-life encounter arise. Once the human heart rises over about 150 beats per minute (bpm) we naturally revert to our most basic of instincts, almost caveman-like. As a martial artist, part of my training is to work with this physiological dynamic to build up the ability to naturally carry the subtle and elaborate martial skills over into potential extreme conditions. Composure is vital to be highly effective. We term this 'pressure testing'.

Part of this pressure testing is obvious on one level and subtle on another. When an army goes to war, soldiers use a battle cry as a way to motivate themselves and elicit fear in their enemy. It also helps override the flight and freeze response and directs all available physiological resources into fight mode.

What is less well-known about the battle cry is that the most feared warriors throughout history would also use a form of it after the event. They would release all the fear they had to suppress in order to fight. This would be the time when they would allow their tears to come to the surface. This process was encouraged and it could take minutes, hours or even days to work through. In ancient cultures such as Sparta, this was not seen as a weakness; it was seen as absolutely necessary for making soldiers effective for battle time and time again. A soldier had to resolve his trauma and process his fear in battle to be free of doubt for his next encounter.

I believe that Zeigarnik's observations and Kübler-Ross's five stages help us understand how we need effective ways to process information and emotions in day-to-day life. We innately seek to close loops, yet people mistakenly reach for mental stimulation and escape mechanisms when it is closure that they long for. This confusion creates distress. They are looking for the wrong thing in the wrong place. Then to compound the problem, when we realise it isn't working, we are taught to feel guilty about having the problem. Then we are expected to try harder through the perceptual filter of guilt! Phew...even thinking about it is tiring for me.

2. When We Look Back, We Think Could We Have Somehow Done Better.

> "All men choose what they perceive to be the good choice at every moment; however, they have no way of knowing if what they are choosing is actually good, or destructive."
>
> SOCRATES

There is a belief that permeates society that can be described as a very special form of insanity. This is buying into the idea that guilt and blame are actually useful. What raises this to the level of insanity is that scientifically, although we have the words 'guilt' and 'blame' in the dictionary and in our vocabulary, they have no foundation...zero!

I listened to an interview some years back where an explorer was sharing his experience of venturing deep into the unchartered Amazon when he discovered what might prove to be the last of the indigenous tribes. He explained that there is a structured protocol for whenever this type of engagement occurs. The exploration team has to undergo rigorous health screening to ensure there is no danger of contaminating the tribe with strains of disease that are part of our daily immune system but that could be deadly to them. The team would be made up of various experts with one of them being a top-notch translator. Step by step the translator would build up a path of communication by systematically building a dictionary of words starting with the basics such as 'ground' and 'sky'. After months of rigorous work, the explorer and his team got to an impasse over the word 'mistake'. What became apparent was that the tribe could not understand the concept of a mistake. It made absolutely no sense to them. It was as if modern man had invented it.

At this point, you might find that your mind can come up with a whole list of mistakes as mine did upon hearing this. Please hold on though as this will make sense soon.

As per the Socrates quote on the previous page, we know what we know and don't know what we don't. At any moment in time, we cannot know what we don't know. There's the elusive obvious at work again.

However, we find that we, in the modern educated world of cars, gold bars and voyages to Mars, actually believe that a mistake is somehow possible. By buying into a word, we have bought into something deeper.

You might wonder where I am going with this. Well, fiction has its uses as it taps into the creative mind but it's not always useful in learning as often it just adds another layer of confusion. To believe we can go back into the past and do something better than we originally did is the flip side of saying that we can go into the future and bring back the winning lottery numbers. Neither are possible. We get a linguistic hint when this insanity is at play when we hear the word 'should'. 'I should have x, y or z' is physically impossible unless you have H.G Wells's time machine handy.

So if a 'mistake' is impossible, could 'guilt' and 'blame' also be impossibilities? I believe this is so.

At this point, you might be thinking something like this: 'if people didn't acknowledge mistakes, feel guilt, or apportion blame, they would never learn and there would be no improvement'. I totally understand this but I also see that sometimes the scales of justice seem to work and other times they don't. There is so much confusion over the use of punishment as an effective learning and teaching mechanism. It looks very hit and miss to me.

If we stop buying into the possibility that mistakes, guilt and blame are real, how can we effectively move forward?

> We should not look back unless it is to derive useful lessons from past errors, and for the purpose of profiting by dearly bought experience.
>
> GEORGE WASHINGTON

I really like Washington's quote especially the words 'dearly bought experience'. The word 'errors' doesn't sit so well with me but maybe he was simply applying words that we generally understand. I would like to replace 'errors' with 'decisions' simply as it is more truthful and scientifically sound.

If we have always done our best in every moment and we accept that we cannot change the past, then the wise choice is to invest in the 'dearly bought experience' that sits below every 'error' we have ever made. Later on, we will see how you can improve your ability to learn from the past by having **words work for us** rather than us working for them. This will make use of some very simple yet elaborate hypnotic dynamics.

What I would like to share now is something that might help to start the process of taking out the judgement that comes from applying words like error, mistake, guilt and blame. It might be worth considering that whenever a person uses these words, they are in a state of **confusion.**

One thing that can loosen the underlying resistance that comes from this confused state is reviewing the four stages of competency. This concept helps us see that no one has ever been successful in anything without incompetence yet if you call someone incompetent in Scotland, you'd better be ready to run like the clappers or stand and fight your ground. It is generally considered an insult. If however we follow the four stages, we can see that incompetence is so neutral a word that it could also be taken as a compliment. It would signify that someone is **intelligent.**

So what I would propose is that you consider the idea that **'incompetence is a skill that can lead to greater skills'.**

I will place this into a useful context later.

If we have always done our best in every moment and we accept that we cannot change the past, then the wise choice is to invest in the 'dearly bought experience' that sits below every error **(decision)** we have ever made. Later on, we will see how we can improve our ability to learn from the past in a very natural way.

3. We Believe That Trying Harder Is The Solution.

More likely than not, this belief was probably installed during our school days. School taught us a great deal more than the content of the curriculum.

One reason for this belief may be because teachers cannot give children very much individual attention. Back in 2011, data showed that Britain's primary schools averaged about 19.9 pupils per teacher compared to the European average of 14.5, according to the EU's statistical agency Eurostat. Lithuania and Denmark have fewer than 10 pupils per teacher, Poland 10.2 and Italy 10.7. I don't have scientific data to prove this, but my intuition says that there is a direct relationship between class sizes and teachers giving students the 'must try harder' message. I truly believe that if the teachers had the time and opportunity, they would be only too willing to provide children with the assistance they need in order to fully understand the concepts they're being taught. Such learning would stand students in good stead both at school and in later life. But the curriculum, passing exams and the educational institution itself mostly skips over this kind of learning.

In Daoism it is seen that there are two distinct parts to learning. One is teaching and the other is education. Although separate, the two parts are intertwined like the human DNA helix. We can see that it is possible that teaching itself is an education. This is maybe why great teachers know that they learn as much or maybe more than they teach.

When a class size increases, the stretching of resources creates a greater need for children to conform and generalise just to get through the curriculum. There is not enough time and space for the teacher pupil relationship to develop the underlying fundamentals that come with 'learning how to learn'.

One fundamental is assisting a child to recognise what they are 'naturally good at'. Back in their nursery days, a child may have played with a toy where plastic shapes are pushed, squeezed or hammered through a template with holes cut out to match the shapes. There would be an assortment of triangles, squares, stars, circles, etc. The aim of the toy is to teach the child that a square peg doesn't fit so well in a round hole, no matter how hard they hammer it.

Yet, when the same child grows up, they often find that their whole life is about hammering away to fit themselves into a world which doesn't quite match the shape of their natural abilities.

Sure, lots of people will have some parts in their life where they feel totally absorbed in what they do as they feel so well aligned that they experience their eustress zone. The same people however often cannot wait for a vacation to come about as it feels like the hammer is in someone else's hand.

I believe that when a teacher is able to listen to a pupil and what makes that pupil tick as a growing and unfolding person, it has a positive effect on the eventual shape that this child's character will take. The aim is to uncover and discover more of their true nature, and acquire the skill of casting their nets wide to gain experience while also being able to hone in on what is worth allocating their time, resources and informed enthusiasm towards. Without this understanding, there is the potential that as they progress through life they'll fall into the trap of being a 'Jack of all trades but master of none'.

A second fundamental that children pick up more through interactions rather than through direct teaching is the ability to ask 'quality questions'. It is possible that a level of intelligence in the human world is primarily based on the ability to ask questions that are both efficient and effective. It is also possible that in the post-school environment, an adult's quality of life will be almost 100% in proportion to the quality of questions a person asks of themselves and others. When a child and teacher have the time for one-to-one dialogue, this is where the ability to ask quality questions can be developed and can assist in fostering a creative learning mindset that will be invaluable whenever life presents challenges.

One simple way to bring these two fundamentals together is to start discerning the following:

a. What is taught and learned that works for people **generally**.
b. What is taught and learned that works for them as an **individual**.

This is a basic understanding of the contrast between content and context. For example, children are often taught 'fighting is bad' and in many contexts we can agree that it is. However, if a child is being bullied or is standing up for a friend or sibling, we might want to reconsider. Some will say that physically defending themselves is appropriate and others will say that it is not. I am not saying whether fighting is justified or not. I'm simply showing that one tiny piece of additional information can shift a decision one way or another.

This is a key part of the drama that unfolds in *Twelve Angry Men*, one of my father's favourite movies. If you haven't seen it, it's a black and white classic where the lead role is played by the late Henry Fonda. The plot involves a Hispanic teenager who is accused of murder with all the evidence pointing to his guilt. Fonda and 11 other men retire to the jury room for what should be an open and shut case. Fonda is not certain of the boy's guilt and urges the other jurors to at least work through the evidence and test each piece for reliability. A guilty verdict would send the boy to his death, despite his age. As they carefully consider the evidence, it becomes clear that things are not how they initially appeared. As the evidence is broken down and re-evaluated, each juror comes to see how they had projected their own lives onto the trial and this leads to unexpected discoveries about their own characters.

Bear this movie in mind and now think back to the 'fighting is bad' example. I've been a martial artist for more than 30 years and one of my mantras is 'my response to a fighting situation will be appropriate and proportionate'. You might ask what this is and in all honesty I do not know. The conditions at the time have always dictated that and will continue to do so. So is fighting bad? If you say yes or no, I invite you to consider that somewhere in your education, the contrast between 'what works generally' and 'what works individually' was not consciously covered very clearly. You might well be too caught up in the content (fighting) in your own mind to see the context (the actual situation).

What I would say here before I progress further is that although I have noted class size as being a factor in pupils not getting enough individual attention, the reality is contextual. There is probably a mixture of factors. So it is just a generalisation to assist with seeing one of many potential underlying reasons. A class size of 12 could be ideal for one teacher but not so good for another. It is all **contextual.**

When we try harder, it is usually a reaction from a confused mind which believes that doing anything is better than nothing. Although based on good intentions, it is easy to push too far, creating a see-saw effect with another problem springing into place on the other side of the solution. For example, people who are trying to quit smoking often end up with a new addiction, such as over-eating. That 'must try harder' mentality can then lead to a sense of hopelessness and giving up on learning and self-development. Trying harder takes a lot of effort and too often eventually leads to what is deemed as failure.

We need a different way of thinking if we are to solve the problems we have created. We need to work smarter rather than harder.

> We cannot solve our problems with the same thinking we used to create them.
>
> ALBERT EINSTEIN

This quote is so useful that this is the second time I have used it and, as it is fundamental to applying leverage, it won't be the last time you encounter it. People do themselves a great disservice when they think they can outsmart nature. The reality is that we need to tap into nature more. Remember once again the table in Figure 4 and the million to one ratio between the subconscious and conscious mind? Trying to impose your way on the subconscious is about as wise as trying to lift yourself off the ground by your bootlaces.

This type of thinking compounds over time and we end up with a mind tied up in knots: it is trying to use the same method of thinking that created a long-term state of confusion to get out of the confusion.

In Chapter 2.2, we will learn how to use a simple and secret de-hypnosis technique to tap into our inner wisdom. This way we will stay grounded in our ability to learn efficiently from our valuable life experience despite the increasing pace of the modern world. Life's challenges will more and more only faze us only momentarily.

Summary

- We can get so engrained in our habitual nature that we become blind to what is right in front of us.

- Trying harder when you are already confused just leads to more confusion.

- Humans naturally seek closure; give yourself time to process thoughts and emotions.

In the next chapter we will build on what we've learned from separating stress into distress and eustress and take it to another level with a simple de-hypnosis technique.

> Supreme excellence consists in breaking the enemy's resistance without fighting.
>
> SUN TZU

Aim — Using a combination of hypnosis-based dynamics, we'll create a communication channel with the mind that makes for more coherence. We won't need to go to war with ourselves to bring about beneficial change.

Concepts

1 The Levnosis Attitudes.

2 The 'What Works' linguistic dynamics.

3 Fractionation mode and defractionation mode.

4 The Autopilot Tool.

5 The Automicity Tool.

6 The Perfect Pause

Chapter 2.2

Finding The Hypnotic Path Of Least Resistance

I was somewhere around the age of 10 when my interest in bicycles stopped being purely about fun and became more of a mini business venture. I used the earnings from my newspaper delivery round to buy used bikes, interchange parts to make enhancements, and sell the bikes on at a profit. It wasn't easy money, the work was often quite taxing and I also had to invest money in my toolkit. Sure, I could borrow some tools from my dad and friends but as more bikes were upgraded, I needed to be more professional.

One task that I learned a lot from was when I replaced the leather seat and seat post on a racing bike. The predicament came when I loosened the nuts and bolt assembly that gripped the frame around the circular post but the seat post would not shift. It was stuck solid. I added some oil that would normally be used for lubricating a chain and bearings but that didn't help either.

I was about to give up when I remembered the mechanic my dad took his car to. I washed cars for him occasionally as he also had a wedding car rental business and needed extra hands when things got really busy. As I knew Derek pretty well, I challenged him with a 'bet you can't sort this one out' approach in the hope it would be enough to distract him from his paid work. He reached for an oil can, and I immediately knew this was special stuff because he produced it with all the mystery and gravitas of a fakir revealing a bottle with a magic genie inside. Derek applied the oil and told me to come back the next day.

I had already tried oil so I doubted it would work. But when I returned as directed, the post was out of the frame. I was happy yet also somewhat confused and even perturbed. He then revealed his secret. He taught me how there are many different oils for different applications whether it be bicycle chains or even engine oil. There was a grade of oil called 'easing oil' which was specifically engineered to penetrate deep into the areas that lubrication type oils could not. All he did was apply some easing oil and let it do its work over a few hours. Then he was able to turn the post back and forward just a millimetre or so. He repeated this several times with just a bit more movement back and forwards until eventually the oil penetration and the freeing motion allowed the post to come free.

For me this was a great example of the contrast between working hard and working smart. Applying easing oil, patiently allowing it the time to do the job it was designed to do plus some manual assistance to help it work its way in, was almost too easy.

This chapter will help you apply easing oil to your thinking; by using a incremental approach you will be able to make effective changes in your daily habitual thinking.

I would like you to consider an idea. I briefly introduced a word earlier in this book that you may or may not recall. The word was 'coherence'. I will expand on coherence and its usefulness later; for now, it would be helpful to allow your mind to hold in mind my story about easing oil as this is the way that coherence works.

To help you do this, we'll start a way of communicating between the conscious and subconscious mind that will allow us to learn from the underlying resistance of the habits that make trouble for us.

What we want to consider is that no matter how negatively a bad habit affects our lives now, the underlying intention of the habit is a positive one...misguided... but positive. The misguided element comes from mistaking what was a useful habit at the outset for one that is still useful today. We missed the point where life progressed, and the habit lost its usefulness.

The realisation that a habit is no longer useful is potential energy just waiting to be utilised. This is the case no matter how long the habit has been held onto after it had lost its usefulness. The trick for us is to separate out the valuable information from the emotional resistance.

In this context it is the duty of learning to help bring closure to the underlying intention of the habit. This is brought about by revealing the **understanding** it brings which allows it to be energetically released by the mind. It's the conscious mind getting the unconscious lesson and finally being able to let go of the past.

You will already be doing this to some degree in your life but we want to nudge it from being a possibility that may occur into a probability that you will make happen.

The incremental and gradual alignment of the conscious and subconscious (which we are calling coherence) will be achieved by:

1. Following Einstein's idea of shifting our thinking away from that which created the problem.
2. Striking a balance between knowledge and experience.
3. Applying some ideas from a variety of hypnosis dynamics. These will help us reduce resistance and then facilitate change that works for us.

As noted already, the study of hypnosis is aimed at communicating effectively with the subtle aspects of the human mind, especially the crossover between the conscious and subconscious mind. In some fields of hypnosis, this is called the Critical Factor and its role is to choose what we'll internalise from the outside world. It is sometimes described as a guard at the gates deciding which people to let in and which people to keep out. The problem is that the guard is usually so busy and distracted with data overload that he unwittingly allows in some unwelcome guests. He usually does a very good job, but when he's tired his attention slips and all kinds of riff-raff get past the gates. It can take a lot time and effort to evict them later on.

Soon, we will look at how we can help the guard tidy things up through using the spring clean idea. It's like providing the guard with high-quality rest and nutrition so he is even more effective when he gets back to work. Not only will he be able to keep up with his usual job at the gate but he'll also be able to identify the gatecrashers and show them the door. When the guard's rested and refreshed, he'll make better decisions over what to let in and what to keep out, more of the time.

Before moving to the next section, I want to consciously activate your subconscious mind and its hypnotic dynamics with just one more analogy about the benefits of working smart rather than working hard. It will help make the coherence idea more tangible as we progress through this chapter.

I used to supplement my living as an electrical technician by working on small domestic projects such as installing additional sockets or connecting up new cookers or showers. It was less mentally demanding than my technical day job but was usually more hard work physically. On one occasion I had to drill into some brickwork and, despite trying various masonry drill bits, I was getting nowhere because the bricks were so hard. I called a buddy who was always a great source of knowledge and he asked me if I had tried the hammer setting on my drill. I thought he was playing a prank on me - I was asking about drills and he was talking hammers. I hesitantly went back to the drill and there was a switch with a very faint symbol of a hammer on it. I just hadn't noticed it before (a perfect example of me crossing over from unconscious incompetence to conscious incompetence!). I activated the hammer mode, gently pulled the trigger, and as the bit rotated, there was a slightly different sound. As I applied the drill to the masonry, it went through the brickwork with ease. There was a lot of noise and the dust went everywhere but it did the job. I owed my buddy a beer for sure.

It was the same tool that did the work but the hammer mode allowed both the drilling and hammer action to work together. The hammer mode allowed an oscillation effect that is not too far from the easing oil dynamic. I will introduce you to a way to apply these ideas to your own thinking as we progress.

1. Levnosis - The Fulcrum Point

I want to introduce a new word for the Critical Factor which monitors the bridge between the conscious and subconscious and that word is **levnosis**, an interplay of the words leverage and hypnosis. It underlines the fact that ideas from hypnosis provide a useful pivot point between the conscious and subconscious. Levnosis will help bring our conscious and subconscious into alignment and its ultimate aim is to improve the quality of our lives and those around us.

The hypnosis-based ideas that make up levnosis are shown in Figure 6 and, while they might not hold the same level of tangible truth as gravity, there is truth within them that makes them extremely useful. I do not ask you agree to any of them. I only ask that you try them on for size and see if they work for you as you work through the chapters.

FIGURE 6

Levnosis Attitudes

I. The secret that isn't a secret is that all improvement comes from doing more of what works for you, less of what doesn't, or a combination of both.

II. When the conscious and subconscious minds are in alignment we have no problems, only solutions.

III. The subconscious mind is impressed by true effort.

IV. We notice what is different but are attracted towards the familiar.

V. You become what you practice.

VI. Practice transforms a skill into a habit.

VII. All changes are infinitesimally small; we just don't notice them until they reach a certain size.

VIII. Solutions are always multidimensional.

IX. Solutions don't come until we are ready for them.

X. We are always on autopilot to a degree. All we can really do is build a better one.

What you will discover is that all of the 10 items above are being applied in this book on the conscious and subconscious levels. Some will be more conscious and obvious; others will remain below your radar. This chapter will be more consciously directed towards item ii.

In Part 0, we discussed how the wider the divide between the conscious and subconscious aspects of our mind, the more problems we experience. For example, at some point you may have experienced buyer's remorse, not because the item was defective or anything like that but because you just can't understand why you bought the damn thing.

I remember buying a shirt and even before I got home I was kicking myself because I knew it wasn't right for me. Luckily I was able to return it but I couldn't fathom what had driven me to buy it in the first place. It was as though my conscious desires and subconscious needs were on completely different wavelengths. So how do we begin to close the gap between the conscious and subconscious minds?

> The more trust we gain with our inner self, the better chance we have of seeing through all those black and grey lies.

Before we get into that, let's take a quick look at lies. Institutions, such as the FBI, categorise lies as white, grey and black. A white lie is where the person does not have any bad intent and is in fact being thoughtful. One example is 'of course Santa is real!' At the other extreme there is the black lie where someone denies their guilt in order to protect their position. Grey lies are the most common and are the trickiest for a lie detector because they are often a mixture of true and false. Some use a play on words to work around their denial; Bill Clinton tried this with the American public when he denied his relationship with a certain intern. And he succeeded... but only for a very brief time. The lie eventually led to his downfall as US President.

In these modern times, the availability of data and information has never been greater and shows no sign of slowing down. The sheer amount of it and its ready availability makes it harder to spot the truth. Therefore discerning who or what to place our trust in becomes even more crucial. The marshmallow experiment showed us that trust was critical for the children taking part in the study and trust is just as important for adults. The more trust we can gain with our own inner self, the better chance we have of effectively seeing through all those black and grey lies.

So how do we create more trust in our inner selves?

I think it would be a good idea at this point to share how we generally become confused. This is where an example could be useful. Derren Brown, a UK-based entertainer, has become well-known internationally because of the masterly way he integrates hypnosis, suggestion, cold reading, misdirection, and showmanship. In one TV programme, he showed just how much we are influenced by the outside world. He did this by challenging two top marketing experts to design a poster for a pet cemetery. He met them in a conference room in a London hotel, explained their task and then left them for a couple of hours. Just before he left, he put a sealed envelope in the middle of the conference table. It would be opened later.

When he returned, the marketers broke into big smiles as they showed Derren their final version. They were delighted with their great idea. The poster showed a big cuddly bear standing in St Peter's place beside the Pearly Gates.

Then Derren played his hand. The marketers' grins disappeared when they saw an almost 100% identical version emerge from the sealed envelope in the middle of the table. They couldn't fathom how this could have happened.

Derren asked them to watch some footage. He played the two men a movie in which they had played the starring roles. It had been secretly filmed and showed the two marketers travelling from their London office to the hotel only hours earlier. A host of images had been planted all along the carefully planned route. They aimed to install a series of images in the men's short-term memory and so lead their design decisions. This even included a person carrying a toy bear past the marketers as they entered the hotel. Finally Derren said he was simply demonstrating to them what advertisers do to the unsuspecting public each and every day.

With this example alone it is no surprise therefore that confusion over what to believe and what not to believe is so prevalent. As the subconscious is so automatic, we can never totally control what we allow into our minds but we can take a measure of control by systematically learning to:

a. Raise our awareness of what signals we receive from the outer world and ourselves to know we have been on autopilot for a period of time. For example, finding yourself arriving at a destination and despite being 'awake' on the journey, sensing that your mind was not present for part of it. The signal is simply that you are aware that you cannot fully recall part of the journey.
b. Develop insight as to what triggers us to experience our individual autopilot.
c. Mindfully scheduling daily time slots when autopilot is turned off by using hypnosis dynamics to help us gain insight into our habitual thinking.
d. Notice how we can then incrementally improve the ability and quality of our autopilot so it makes us less susceptible to buying into what the world would have us believe is good for us despite what our personal evidence says.

Discernment: Chipping Away At Whatever Doesn't Add Quality To Your Life

Discernment is the skill that allows all of the above points to be developed. If you look in a dictionary, you will find that there is very little information on the meaning of this word other than 'the act of discerning'. What I found when looking for synonyms was 'insight' which feels right for me.

I will expand on applying discernment in much more detail in Part 4. Earlier on I said: "this book will help you use the chisel of your inner discernment to chip away at what you carry around that doesn't align with your true nature, the source of every problem you currently perceive." Without your inner discernment, the chisel is using you.

Discernment is what helps us see through the confusion of mixed messages that make up the grey lies or what may be better termed 'fallacies' - the things that do not work for us but are still applied because of the subconscious mind's priority, keeping you safe even if that means staying confused.

Discernment is the ability to judge well, the ability to tell the difference between truth and falsehood. It has two elements to it, what works for us (subjective) and what works for other people (objective). Sometimes these align and sometimes they do not.

Discernment however is itself tricky in that it is less of a cause and more of an effect. Our state of coherence determines the quality of our discernment. If your conscious and subconscious are in conflict, maybe due to fatigue, discernment is more based on memories of what worked for us in the past or what generally works for other people. It lacks the wisdom that presence and subjectivity brings us.

You've probably already guessed my favourite quote of all time: Einstein's comment on 'not being able to solve a problem without shifting your thinking'. My second favourite is:

> God grant me the serenity to accept the things I cannot change, courage to change the things I can, and the wisdom to know the difference.
>
> REINHOLD NIEBUHR

In my opinion, the third part of the quote holds the key to discernment because I don't believe that wisdom is mystical. I believe that wisdom is the result of a coherent state where the conscious and subconscious are so well aligned and the choices offered are so useful that solutions come easily. The solutions feel so obvious that people often ask themselves 'why didn't I see this earlier?'

Levnosis will assist in bringing more coherence into your life. We will come back to coherence again later.

For now, before we take a detailed look at autopilot and automicity, which I introduced briefly in Chapter 0.2, I would like to finish this section by emphasising that we cannot turn off our autopilot completely as it is part of the link between our mind and body. Even when you sleep deeply, an unusual noise picked up by your ever watchful subconscious can wake you. So although it cannot be switched off, what we can do is take a measure of control. By creating coherence between the conscious and subconscious, we get a glimpse into the truth of our true nature. As the subconscious is a million to one times more influential than the conscious mind is on our habitual thinking, the briefest glimpse into its nature on a regular basis is incredibly helpful for assisting us to break free of habits that hold us back.

Autopilot And Automicity For Your Toolbox

In Chapter 0, I shared a personal example of autopilot on autopilot when I ended up parking my car in someone else's drive. This was an example which had no real consequences (except my blushes) but life is not always so kind. I will now share another two examples.

Autopilot example no.2:
It was reported by the British media in September 2013 that on the 13th of August 2013 an incident report revealed that both pilots on an Airbus passenger plane were asleep at the same time within a UK-operated aircraft flying on autopilot.

One of the pilots indicated in a report to the Civil Aviation Authority (CAA) that the pair nodded off after both had only five hours' sleep over the previous two nights.

The incident report further noted: "We don't know why the pilots had had so little sleep before this flight. They were taking it in turn to have rest periods, with the one always checking the autopilot and it looks as if both fell asleep at the same time."

This incident caused many people within this global industry to share a number of similar examples. Fortunately, none of these incidents contributed to accidents and the learnings were directed at how changes in flight technology had at times led to changes in flight scheduling that did not allow for sufficient rest periods.

This is what I would call having autopilot on autopilot: advances in technology tried to ignore the basic human risk of fatigue and the need for adequate rest. Fortunately no one was hurt.

Autopilot example no.3:
Some years back, I watched a fascinating Discovery Channel documentary on the sinking of the Titanic. The programme revealed how a series and combination of factors led to the Titanic sinking on its maiden voyage. The most intriguing factor for me was the rudder design, which was described as the Titanic's Achilles heel.

The training for the ship's crew missed a very important factor on how the ship, some 852 feet long, might turn in an emergency or avoid collision with another

> ...autopilot itself is not fundamentally bad; it is just that when it is compounded by forces such as fatigue or pseudo competence, it can lead to consequences which we would prefer to avoid.

vessel or an iceberg. The response to the sighting of the iceberg (which itself was late due to another technical oversight) meant that the crew had responded in their usual way, which you might find to be the wisest choice based on common sense. They shut down the engines immediately and steered away from the direction of the iceberg as fast as humanly possible. This unfortunately made the rudder less effective. Its innovative design was such that the faster the ship travelled, the more steer could be developed from the rudder. If they had sped up instead and then steered away from the iceberg, they would have missed it completely.

This is what I would call having autopilot on autopilot due to the ship's staff having a lack of technical awareness and inadequate training. Also, people reverting back to what they assume to be the right course of action when in an extremely stressful situation. As you are probably aware, this tragically led to the loss of many lives.

We can see that the consequences of all three examples were each very different. What we can say is that autopilot itself is not fundamentally bad; it is just that when it is compounded by forces such as fatigue or pseudo competence, it can lead to consequences which we would prefer to avoid.

Look back briefly to example no.2. Aircrafts have an autopilot facility that lets the pilots rest between take-off and landing, the most demanding parts of the flight. If this mechanism is used to improve alertness when the pilots most need it, it's a good thing. If used to replace the need for sleep, it's a bad thing. Cars are often fitted with cruise control to make long motorway journeys easier on the legs and feet. So autopilot has many uses.

To repeat the point: the problem is when our own autopilot is on autopilot. These are the times when we are struggling so hard to do everything that's expected of us that we skim through life, barely touching the surface; we're certainly not grounded in our minds, bodies, thoughts or feelings. It's like treading water. We're so focused on keeping our head above the waterline that we keep finding ourselves ending up in the same problematic situations over and over again without having any idea how we got there.

If we look closely, we can see that the experience of autopilot on autopilot is very similar to a complex hypnotic trance that we could not create consciously. We could in theory make it more likely to occur by denying ourselves adequate sleep such as that experienced by the airline pilots in the example. Even then, numerous scenarios and factors need to come together and that is tricky to do deliberately.

What I will offer however is an autopilot experience that will give us an idea of how the mind's dynamics respond in an automated fashion when we ask specific questions in a structured way.

I will also offer another experience - automicity. This gives us access to a different kind of thinking than the type that gets us into problems because the guard at the gates of our subconscious mind is falling asleep and is allowing all sorts of rubbish to enter.

I will come back to both autopilot and automicity in more detail as we continue through this chapter. There will be a combination of concepts and experiences to tap into both your conscious awareness and subconscious intuition. What will follow now are two dynamics that will be similar on one level of the mind and yet completely different on another. The first of these two dynamics will be applied identically within the autopilot tool and automicity tool. The second of these dynamics will have a common theme but a completely different effect.

Dynamic One: the 'what works' linguistics
This applies a linguistic dynamic based on contrasting 'What Works for You' with 'What Doesn't Work for You'. This will be covered in detail in Section 2 of this chapter.

Dynamic Two: fractionation mode and defractionation mode
This will take you into a dynamic of the human mind which assists with understanding how we learn initially and also how we can naturally create and open up space for new learnings. This will delve into the communication and processing between the conscious and subconscious connection via fractionation and defractionation, two modes of applying the mind. This will be covered in detail in Section 3 of this chapter.

2. The 'What Works' Linguistics

Let's take a look at an element of the elusive obvious that is just too simple for most of us to see or even acknowledge.

I asked some of the most successful people I know two very simple questions:

1. Can you name something you do in your life that works for you?
2. What is an example of something that does not work so well for you?

It amazed me that these successful people still found question two much easier to answer than the first one. And why on earth were such high-fliers still doing something that didn't work for them? Why would a sane person keep doing something that doesn't work for them, especially if they are consciously aware of it?

It seems to me that every one of us is confused and running around on autopilot most of the time, even those who've achieved success. By the way, we call this state 'normal'.

We readily accept the confusion and being on autopilot because we're constantly assessing whether things will bring us more pleasure or more pain. We are continually making deals between short-term pleasures versus long-term pain. This relentless deal making gets very tiring over time. The good news is that we can work with the subconscious mind to help untangle and alleviate this confusion and fatigue.

Now that we've understood basically how our confusion came about, the next step is to look at how different questions have different effects on the mind. 'What works for you?' is a good example of a question that taps into our creativity. Change the question to 'what are you good at?' and quite a different effect is created. The question feels more personal and even judgemental. It could lead us to confuse our behaviour with our identity if we were not mindful of the mechanics and energetics of linguistics.

The most effective way to access the subconscious is by directing our communication away from identity and towards behaviour. Doing something good or bad is much more helpful than being labelled as good or bad as it offers useful information for making changes by learning from experience. Questions like 'what works for you?' and 'what doesn't work for you?' open us up and create a shift in mindset. We are less constrained by judgements and the subconscious mind is more willing to play. The subtle shift from 'what are you bad at?' to 'what doesn't work for you?' allows your mind more freedom as it doesn't have to take things so personally and go on the defensive.

As we move from considering 'what works for you?' to 'what doesn't work for you?' or vice versa, it can feel a little like a see-saw tipping from one side to another, perhaps you can almost feel your hands moving up and down like the two pans of a pair of balance scales. This kinaesthetic sensation will become very useful later when we combine it with a hypnotic dynamic.

Bear this in mind: words have power. This power is expanded and compounded when the words are constructed into carefully crafted questions. Arguably, what separates people who learn from their life's ups and downs and those who do not is the quality of the questions they ask themselves. We will apply leverage by making great use of high-quality questions to tap into the amazing wisdom that is available within our subconscious mind.

3. Fractionation Mode And Defractionation Mode

There is a very high possibility that neither fractionation nor defractionation are terms that have ever crossed your path. They are terms that are applied in the field of hypnosis and will assist us greatly when we look later at how to develop automicity to create a more helpful autopilot.

I suggest that first we experience these dynamics and then discuss the contrasting/shifting effect they offer us in helping gain a measure of control over automated thinking.

EXPERIENCE 4: FRACTIONATION MODE AND DEFRACTIONATION MODE

In Experience 2, we used an elastic band to demonstrate distress/eustress zones. We will now expand (no pun intended) on this experience...

Fractionation physical experience - via linear motion
Hold the elastic band between your two hands and take it to where there is no slack.

Now separate your hands by a very small incremental amount. Call this point 1. You will do this 10 times; this will give you an idea of what distance to travel to allow for 10 movements.

Complete another 9 times. Note how this feels.

Now repeat in reverse, this time with the distance between the hands closing (to where there is no slack) with the same incremental feeling with 10 movements. Note how this feels.

Defractionation physical experience - via multidimensional motion
Hold the elastic band between your two hands and take to where there is no slack.

Now separate your hands by a very small amount. Call this point 1. You will do this 10 times.

Release so you move back about halfway between your starting point and Point 1.

Separate your hands again such that you will expand past Point 1.

Repeat for a total of 10 expansions and contractions. Note how this feels. The aim here is to gradually increase the distance between the hands but in a cyclic way.

Now repeat in reverse this time with the distance between the hands closing with the same cyclic feeling. Note how this feels.

When I have guided many different people through this experience, the feedback varies so much that it amazes me. One example was from a friend who is a keep-fit fanatic. She said that the first experience (fractionation) felt like when she planned a workout logically step by step. The second experience (defractionation) felt more like when she went with the flow and let the workout work itself out. Neither one was better than the other, it was more like they both had their place and tuning into which to use at what time was what kept her training well structured yet also flowing. It seemed to increase her intuition.

Another friend said that the first experience was like when he first started fishing; he'd use too much force to catch his fish and would often end up either losing them off the hook or breaking his line. The second experience was more like when he learned that once the fish were on the hook, allowing it to swim away and use up its strength would make it easier when he slowly reeled it in. For some fish he would repeat this action over and over until he eventually brought it in. The fish was less stressed this way and wouldn't take too long to recover before he released it back into the water hoping to compete with it again another day. The skill for him was to catch as big a fish as he could with as thin a fishing line as possible.

No matter how the experience relates to your own life, most people initially think of fractionation and defractionation as opposites. Even the vocabulary leads us to think that. However this is not the case and it is indeed an illusion. They are in fact more like two sides of the same coin in that they contain the same elements but are arranged differently. This is why considering them as '**modes**' can be very helpful. They are related but in a contrasting way.

I'll now share how fractionation and defractionation work. We will not dig too deep here, just enough to strike a balance with the experience that you've just gained and also to help us take this and dynamic 1 ('what works' linguistics) forward into Autopilot and Automicity further along in this chapter.

3.1 The Fractionation Mode Effect

What: Fractionation is a powerful hypnotic technique. When inducing trance states, practitioners have found that by bringing their client in and out of hypnosis at the beginning of the session, the final trance state is much deeper. This allows for the power of suggestion to be amplified as the brainwave states of alpha/theta make a fertile ground and the fractionation brings more theta brainwaves.

One hypnotic induction uses a progressive relaxation technique that is based on fractionation. Some time is taken with tensing up a number of body areas, holding the tension, and then relaxing. This is repeated as a cycle for a set number of times. With fractionation in this context, the length of time is very important and it is critical not to cycle too much.

When the client is physically relaxed, mental fractionation techniques that shift them in and out of various levels of awareness help them go deeper into trance. It's very effective and we'd benefit from using it in our everyday life rather than leaving it for occasional hypnosis sessions.

The Daoists worked with fractionation to improve meditation practice. They would do some light exercise such as Chi Gung and follow it with a meditation session. Then they'd cycle between periods of movement practice and then periods of stillness practice because both benefitted from the other, especially meditation. The shift from movement to stillness and back again allowed practitioners to access deeper states of meditation.

> High Intensity Interval Training is an exercise strategy that alternates short periods of intense anaerobic exercise with less intense recovery periods. It is also an example of fractionation.

Once you start looking, you'll find fractionation in all sorts of places. For example High Intensity Interval Training (HIIT) is a form of exercise strategy that alternates short periods of intense anaerobic exercise with less intense recovery periods. HIIT sessions may last anywhere between four to 30 minutes. These short, intense workouts boost athletic capacity and condition as well as improving glucose metabolism. I've tried many of these sessions and the type that works best for me is the Tabata regimen which grew out of Professor Izumi Tabata's study of Olympic speed skaters. The regime uses cycles of 20 seconds of ultra-intense exercise followed by 10 seconds of rest, repeated continuously for four minutes (eight cycles). I am now doing less exercise each week but have gained more agility, anaerobic capacity and a huge improvement in my recovery time ability.

In my opinion, fractionation and its positive effect on mental focus is part of the reason for HIIT's effectiveness. I also believe that eustress has a part to play as I now get in 12 minutes what used to take more like one to two hours of training. My body also gets more rest and less wear and tear.

Dynamic: It may be useful to share a brief idea of the effect of fractionation on the human mind. Fractionation leads to what I would describe as an inertia effect. This will probably not make much sense at this stage but hopefully will once you have completed this chapter.

I feel this inertia every time I write a list, including shopping lists. The first two or three items take a bit of thinking about then it's as if there's a tipping point and I can rattle off a dozen items quicker than I can write them down. My mind gets a bit impatient with me for not being physically quick enough to keep up with it.

Fractionation also has a deepening effect. The punishment that I most disliked at school was lines. I don't know if it is only Bart Simpson and myself who experienced this mild form of torture but it did have the desired effect on me - although maybe not the one the teacher planned. I got much better at hiding my mischief. The repetition of the lines would eventually become so automatic that my mind would drift off. Quite ironic as not paying attention was what I was being punished for.

The fractionation effect on the subconscious is less about 'access' and more about 'adding to' and so is very useful in certain contexts. If, for example, I were to ask you 'what are your top 10 favourite movies of all time?' this would create a fractionation dynamic and your top 10 would not only be revealed to me but the exercise of naming them would also re-enforce them in your subconscious. So your top 10 would become more solidified in your mind. This is a useful way to apply fractionation.

Here's a question that I learned from one of my favourite school teachers. It's simple and yet also very wise. He said that he wished for only one thing as a teacher and that was that each day we would leave school and ask ourselves 'what did I learn today that was useful?'

Fractionation however is not so useful for making informed decisions. As fractionation adds inertia to our thinking, it tends to get pulled into memory and so it is more influenced by what has worked for us in the past rather than what is best for us now. In essence it restricts the quality of choice.

What we can say then is that **fractionation assists re-enforcement**. This will help us understand the workings of the automatic pilot dynamic later on.

3.2 The Defractionation Mode Effect

What: Defractionation describes the way the human mind sometimes processes data by moving backwards and forwards between different types of information. This motion acts like a brake, it slows down our thinking. This prevents the mind from taking the easy and habitual path back into memory. This braking effect amplifies clarity and induces the brainwave states of alpha and beta.

This clarity is similar to when a single vital piece of information is given to us and cuts through our confusion; the light bulb goes on. A simple yet common example is where a person is trying to remember someone's name and the harder they try, the more it eludes them. Then when they decide to move onto thinking of something else, up pops the name.

Another example where defractionation is experienced is when a person realises they are driving too fast and close to the car in front. They slow down and only minutes later pass an accident where two cars have collided. A wake-up call like this often allows them to take stock and re-evaluate their priorities e.g. get somewhere fast or get there in one piece?

Dynamic: The dynamic of defractionation is only very subtly different from fractionation for most people when directly compared. Later when it is combined with the 'what works' dynamic to create automicity, it will become more tangible. The linear step-by-step type of movement of fractionation is replaced with constant movement with the tiniest of micro pauses where there is a change of direction. The pause is so small that it is rarely detectible. What we can say is that in Experience 3 the physical distance between the overall end points in fractionation and defractionation were the same. What is less obvious is that the journey is quite different as the movement is linear for fractionation but is non-linear for defractionation and obviously the latter takes a longer period of time overall.

You might find that fractionation and defractionation are not easy to physically distinguish as they are like heads and tails of the same coin. So if you don't see a difference, don't be concerned. What I guarantee you is that your brainwaves are different for each experience, it is just very subtle.

A Metaphor About The Defractionation Effect...
A woman entered a clinical hypnotist's office and before even sitting in the chair to reveal the trauma of her life, she had already broken into uncontrollable tears. The hypnotist sitting behind his desk jumped to his feet and said firmly: "Excuse me! Your session hasn't even started yet!" The woman was so shocked, she immediately stopped crying and apologised profusely as she wiped away the tears with a handkerchief and composed herself. The hypnotist then explained that if he could stop her crying by simply introducing a shock or surprise, she arguably could choose to move on past the relationship that she had been holding onto for so many years.

He explained that it was not an unconscious hypnosis session she needed, it was the conscious understanding that she was punishing herself with the idea that reliving the past was somehow going to bring closure.

The hypnotist simply surprised the woman out of her habitual thinking (fractionation) just enough for her to see what was really going on. She had been used to people listening to her story. They did it with the best of intentions but were actually helping her make the story more permanent, more tragic and part of her personal identity. They had been providing fractionation in response to her fractionation when it was really defractionation she needed so that she could learn to move on.

The defractionation effect is very different to fractionation as inertia is removed when the mind is not allowed to run away with itself. What we have instead is a light level of back and forward movement, an oscillation mode which has a braking effect. This will make much more sense later when experienced as part of automicity.

What we can say is that **defractionation assists re-evaluation**. This will come in very helpful when we look at the automicity dynamic later.

> ...defractionation assists re-evaluation.

Before we move into Section 4 and look at autopilot as a tool, I want to sum up fractionation and defractionation by emphasising that if they feel very much the same at this stage, that is completely understandable and normal.

When I had my experience with drilling the masonry, then switched the mode on the drill to hammer, I noticed a slight shift but it was not obvious. It was only when I physically applied the change of mode to the wall that the effect could really be noticed.

Sections 4 and 5 will show you the real world application of this modality change and that will make it much more tangible for you.

4. The Autopilot Tool

Although we can't create an experience of autopilot on autopilot, we can experience something like autopilot. I will provide a refined version of autopilot later that will give us a hint of how it works so we can get better at recognising what life circumstances lead to it occurring especially where it is not useful.

Three common areas where autopilot can be a hindrance are:

i. When a person is processing a bereavement of some nature.
In Chapter 2.1, we discussed the five stages of loss that people go through. Bear in mind that a major bereavement for one person might not faze another. Although Kübler Ross's model is common to us all, our individuality means that loss affects people very differently and for some people just changing one small habit in their lives can be felt as a deep loss.

ii. When there are too many open loops.
I think this might be best explained with a brief example. One of the most distressing events for many people is moving home. A friend of mine with two young children had a very simple yet effective idea to ease the transition. He hired a storage container and placed in it a large amount of the non-essential furniture which they did not need on a daily basis. He did this over a couple of weeks leading up to the day of the move. The day of the move itself was so easy and slick he vowed that they would never go back to the old way of doing it all in one go. Over the weeks after the move, he gradually emptied the container and filled the new house bit by bit which even allowed some basic decorating to be done without clutter.

We all seem to be able to handle a certain amount of open loops but there's a eustress zone where we have just enough of them open and this brings out the best in us and the daily challenges of life then feel more like opportunities.

iii. Time constraints.
Feeling that there aren't enough hours in the day goes hand in hand with the technological age. The industrial revolution brought many ups and downs and time and motion studies, which assess effectiveness and efficiency, can either help us make wise choices or keep us feeling like a hamster on a treadmill.

A More Refined Autopilot...
Most people I've asked would like an autopilot which brings:

a) Regular and plentiful times to take a healthy break from having to perform and meet targets.

b) An added level of effortlessness to our daily tasks so we can save our vital energy for when it is most needed.

c) A useful way of applying momentum of the mind e.g. when we brainstorm ideas.

d) Learning that has a rhythm to it. One example is where young children learn their maths times tables in a sing-song; the tempo helps them process and remember the data.

e) Particular strategies of applying the mind. One example is an examination strategy that many students now subscribe to. They begin by scanning the examination paper to get a basic understanding of the questions. Then they choose the easier questions and do these first. This allows the mind to gain some momentum by gaining some quick wins. It also gives the subconscious time to start working in the background on the more tricky questions.

f) Where bereavements naturally run their course and memories of shared enjoyable times eventually gain more importance than the loss itself.

We've all had these experiences to some degree. It is just that we would like the leverage to make for more of these so that life feels more in balance. An autopilot that is regularly updated and refined can be of great assistance in bringing about more eustress.

So without further ado, let's test out a way to gain a measure of control and a reference point for our autopilot. We will now experience a refined autopilot where we purposefully integrate the linguistic dynamics of 'what works for you' and 'what doesn't work for you' combined with the fractionation effect.

EXPERIENCE 5: ENGAGE YOUR AUTOPILOT MECHANISM

Here you see four tables; the first two are examples to help you get started.

1. Take a note of the time that you start this exercise.
2. Fill in table 3 with 10 things or experiences that work for you.
3. Now fill in table 4 with 10 things or experiences that don't work for you.
4. Look at the time - how long did it take?

Please note that blank tables can be downloaded from http://www.findingthefulcrum.org.

Tables 1 and 2: _Kieran O'Connor_ (name)

	WHAT WORKS FOR ME
1	Interval exercise training
2	Vegetable smoothies
3	Watching the Discovery Channel
4	Watching TED talks
5	Kung Fu practice
6	Watching rugby and soccer
7	Meditation
8	Eating only when hungry
9	Red wine
10	Power naps

	WHAT DOESN'T WORK FOR ME
1	Getting stuck in traffic
2	Fast food
3	Missing a power nap
4	Watching soap operas
5	Over-training
6	Working overtime
7	Jazz music
8	Very hot weather
9	Low budget movies
10	Spending time with complainers

COMPLETED IN: _10.5 minutes_ (time)

Tables 3 and 4: _____ (name)

WHAT WORKS FOR ME
1
2
3
4
5
6
7
8
9
10

WHAT DOESN'T WORK FOR ME
1
2
3
4
5
6
7
8
9
10

COMPLETED IN: _____ (time)

It's easy for the mind to get stuck in autopilot. When you completed the 'What Works for You' column you may have found that as you wrote down number one, you found it fairly easy to come up with more in that list as there was a link between these answers. This is what it is like to tap into your autopilot. It shows how the mind links one thing to another and aligns with Natural Learning which we covered in Chapter 0.

I don't want to move onto automicity until we are absolutely clear that autopilot is neither good nor bad, it is completely neutral. It is a tool and just like any tool, it has its uses.

Autopilot as a tool will be used much later in Chapter 5.2. We will now contrast what it is to move off autopilot to a degree.

5. The Automicity Tool

As noted earlier, you won't find the word 'automicity' in a dictionary because I made it up; I wanted to create a useful contrast to autopilot. Note that I said 'contrast' and not 'opposite'. This is very important and will become clearer as we continue.

Automicity gives us access to a different style of thinking to the type we used in Experience 5. Automicity will differ from autopilot because it utilises the defractionation mode which assists with re-evaluation. We will discuss this contrast later.

For now, let's gain an experience of the automicity tool as a mechanism for activating areas of the conscious/subconscious connection. The only prerequisite I have is to ask that you leave at least one day's gap between the autopilot experience and the automicity experience. It's a little like drinking water to clean your palate between courses. There is also a more technical reason which will become apparent as we progress.

EXPERIENCE 6: ENGAGE YOUR AUTOMICITY MECHANISM

This exercise is almost the same as Experience 5 except this time please switch between the tables as you fill in each answer. So fill in the first item in the 'What Works for Me' table and then fill in the first line of the 'What Doesn't Work for Me' table.

Please make a note of the time it takes to do this exercise as you did for Experience 5 - you'll generally find this one takes longer. It took me six minutes longer when I did it.

Please note that blank tables can be downloaded from http://www.findingthefulcrum.org.

Tables 1 and 2: *Kieran O'Connor* (name)

	WHAT WORKS FOR ME
1	Rising early from bed
3	Interval training
5	Asking people for help and assistance
7	Power naps
9	Daily still-point meditation
11	Reading a great novel
13	Live comedy shows
15	Ice cold beer after exercise
17	Being out in nature
19	Massage

	WHAT DOESN'T WORK FOR ME
2	Complaining
4	Feeling guilty about the past
6	Eating high carbs
8	Working long hours
10	Bland food
12	Sitting at a PC for long periods
14	Gherkins
16	Lack of sleep
18	Housework
20	The colour pink

COMPLETED IN: *16.5 minutes* (time)

Tables 3 and 4: _____ (name)

WHAT WORKS FOR ME
1
3
5
7
9
11
13
15
17
19

WHAT DOESN'T WORK FOR ME
2
4
6
8
10
12
14
16
18
20

COMPLETED IN: _____ (time)

You will most likely have found this exercise trickier than the autopilot one. It probably took you much longer to complete especially as it is most probably your first time ever consciously. The autopilot experience for me took 10.5 minutes as compared to 16.5 minutes for automicity. You may even have found that you couldn't complete as many of the items because you're not used to this type of experience.

As discussed in Chapter 1.2, when we move from autopilot to automicity it's natural for us to pause more often. Autopilot (via fractionation) is easier because the mind naturally works through association and repetition. Most adults can still rattle off their seven times table at the same tempo as they did as children.

The automicity tool brings together the 'what works' linguistics and the defractionation dynamics. The defractionation aspect naturally takes longer because it's less of a memory-based activity. This type of thinking is more akin to solving a riddle.

> ...when we move from autopilot to automicity it's natural for us to pause more often. Autopilot (via fractionation) is easier because the mind naturally works through association and repetition.

What is worth pointing out is that you might initially be drawn to the list of 20 items (or however many you could achieve this time around). You may look for a way to consciously learn from the list so that you make yourself do more of what works for you and less of what doesn't. This is understandable although not particularly wise - it's a bit like the sailors on the Titanic who instinctively slowed the ship down when they spotted the iceberg. The more you apply automicity, the more you will become aware of the underlying learning that is taking place in the subconscious - this is where the really powerful learning and change takes place.

I'm not trying to dissuade you from making decisions and taking action based on what you learn from the lists, I just want to ensure you understand that these decisions have already benefited from automicity; the wheels have already been set in motion in your subconscious. It is happening below the conscious level, so you will not be aware of the improvements. This is where it pays to put your faith in delayed gratification, because those changes will naturally become more obvious with time.

With automicity working at the subtle levels of the mind, you will in effect switch your mode of thinking so that you will see the wisdom in speeding up when you see the iceberg so that you miss it easily and efficiently. I think Mr Einstein would approve of this shift in thinking.

Automicity = defractionation (oscillating mode dynamic) between the two opposed questions (what works/doesn't work). This helps us dig down into the subconscious and reveal the precious learnings that lie beneath the surface level of associations and habitual mental loops.

Automicity will be used as a tool in Chapter 4.1. For now, let's dig just a little deeper below the surface as you might find that applying automicity will be easier if you understand more about the underlying mechanics.

The red pill or blue pill?

> This is your last chance. After this, there is no turning back. You take the blue pill - the story ends; you wake up in your bed and believe whatever you want to believe. You take the red pill - you stay in Wonderland, and I show you how deep the rabbit hole goes. Remember: all I'm offering is the truth. Nothing more.
>
> MORPHEUS (FROM *THE MATRIX*)

All that talk of the Titanic brings me back to the idea that the subconscious mind is often compared to an iceberg. There is so much hidden below the surface of our everyday selves that it is understandable why Neo in *The Matrix* hesitated before he decided to choose the red pill. To know thyself is not for the faint-hearted. Having read this far, it sounds like the blue pill is not for you either.

For those who haven't seen the first *Matrix* movie, it is the tale of Mr Anderson, a nine-to-five disillusioned computer programmer by day who moonlights as the top-notch software hacker, Neo. He searches for answers and intuitively awaits the mystic, Morpheus, who invites and eventually wakes him up from a perceived reality that is really an elaborate illusion. The red pill awakens him to the fact that he has not been making any true decisions of his own, he has been living within a carefully crafted construct of technology.

The red pill does not have to be a dramatic event as it is in the movie. It can be a gradual process of waking up to yourself each and every day, as you will discover as we progress further.

As automicity is going to prove to be a key aspect of leverage and seeing as we are at a natural fulcrum point in this book, it might be useful to take a break and look at what we have covered so far.

The overall aim of this book is to help us do more of what works for us and less of what doesn't so we find ourselves in our flow more often. It's such a simple idea; yet only when you have a thinking strategy that allows the truth to become more self-obvious, does your inner discernment consciously see it.

In this chapter we are looking at the coherence effect, where the conscious and subconscious become more aligned. This is what we are working towards. The introduction of automicity as a tool will help this come about naturally. What you will discover is that the grey 'lies' start to work themselves out, there is less conflict taking up your energy, and life starts to flow as distress transforms into eustress.

Some of you might have reacted when you read the word 'lies' in the last paragraph. This doesn't mean that you or anyone else is a liar; to call someone a liar is itself a lie. It just means that a behaviour has been confused with an identity. A person who tells lies is potentially open to not lying in the next heartbeat when a new realisation takes place. 'Lies' are simply a form of confusion just waiting for us to wake up with a re-evaluation.
Some of what I share about automicity might appear quite bold, but science backs it up. For instance, automicity works for me and you because of:

a. The Induced Pause Effect
Answers take longer to come when you're using defractionation (automicity) than fractionation (autopilot). There is a lot more pausing induced in automicity. "Okay, but why bother?" you might ask. "Why would I want to take longer in answering a question?" Great question if you don't mind me saying and even better if you are willing to hang on a moment for a response.

In Chapter 1.2, we discussed 'The power of a pause'. This has a number of effects in that when pausing:

  i. We create an 'Alpha Sandwich'. The alpha state is sandwiched between beta states and helps us achieve an overall relaxed yet alert state of mind.
  ii. We gain access to the best of beta and alpha states and this helps us make a better **quality decision**.
  iii. We experience a sweet spot between logic and emotion that improves our decisions. I think this supports my intuition that when we pause to make a decision, we are more in balance. The pause is a kind of pivot point between thinking and feeling.

So although you may not believe that a simple pause can have much of an effect, it's worth noting that in classical physics, Newton's Third Law teaches us that **forces** always come in pairs. For every action, there is an equal and opposite reaction.

To give an example. Barack Obama is considered by many to be one of the world's greatest orators in modern times even to those who do not agree with his politics. Not only are his words very precise and commanding, his real skill is that of 'perfect pausing'. He seems to be able to pause in such a way that eager anticipation is created about what it is to come. When the words arrive, the message they convey is amplified. His pauses skilfully inform and highlight for your subconscious mind what is truly important.

I would like you to consider the idea that all the best choices and decisions you ever made had an equal and opposite force in that there was an element of a **'perfect pause'** that made the space for them to come into being.

The pause comes when we ask a question and wait for an answer. The 'what works' linguistics allow the conscious mind to apply gentle curiosity to the subconscious. We wait, trusting that the subconscious will answer. This is delayed gratification so it follows that the answer feels more satisfying. Delayed gratification gives us the time to look past the symptoms to the cause. There are no guarantees, but the greater the coherence (the sculptor's skills), the more power the discernment tool (the chisel) has to take away that which is not suitable or valuable for us.

b. The path of trust leads to truth
The trust that is created between the conscious and subconscious not only brings more satisfying answers, they also have a greater level of **truth within them**. Truth is dynamic; we update what we believe to be truthful every day, at least to a degree. When you were a child, your parents probably warned you not talk to strangers and that was great advice. Somewhere along the way you will have grown up and realised that talking to strangers is part of getting out into the world. Everyone is a stranger initially. Your parents probably didn't sit you down and specifically spelled this out to you; you will have reached that awareness yourself. What was once a truth was re-evaluated and became a new truth. If 'the truth shall set you free' it would make sense to incrementally **re-evaluate** what works for you and what doesn't.

There's a simple and useful way to practically gauge this. What is very obvious for me is that the things that once bothered me for a long time in the past bother me for less and less time now. Ups and downs are still part of life but I have learned the cognitive skills that turn big potholes into mere speed bumps. I have shared three effects that support automicity. There are many more but we'll leave them for another day. Let us now take a step towards tangible benefits by seeing how the easing oil effect of coherence can help us transform the three basic illusions we introduced earlier.

Automicity Brings Coherence To The Three Illusions

Let's see how applying automicity can shift three of the most basic illusions (discussed in Chapter 2.1) and also how it offers the potential to transform a 'what doesn't work for you' into something that 'does work for you'.

Transforming Illusion 1: We underestimate the need for closure.
When we apply automicity, we discover that the 'what works' question feels gentle and compassionate. We're being kind to ourselves! The oscillation dynamic within defractination helps us process more effectively and we're less likely to get stuck in our habitual thinking. When we re-evaluate, we discover

that **resolution** is indeed more of a by-product of the re-evaluation that's just taken place. Closure becomes more like lots of little steps rather than big, scary, and strenuous ones.

Transforming Illusion 2: When we look back, we think we could have done better.
I think we already know that although automicity won't change the past, it will enable us to make the best of it. By learning and using the automicity tool, you will come to understand why people say 'every cloud has a silver lining'. We discover that bad experiences relax their grip when we actively seek the wisdom within them by communicating with the subconscious in its own language.

Transforming Illusion 3: We believe that trying harder is the solution.
Trying harder is too often like using autopilot to try to get off autopilot. Or finding ourselves in a hole and digging deeper to try and get out of it. Making an effort is a good thing, but it is best if that effort is applied effectively. We now see, for example, how a pause can stop us creating more problems - so that a pause is actually an investment. As you experience and practice automicity, you'll stop digging yourself deeper into trouble and start finding a smarter way out.

If applying automicity assists with these three items, imagine what benefits you could experience by having more coherence, which naturally leads to a greater ability to make informed decisions. It's important to always remember that we don't get anything for nothing. We have to invest our time and effort today to make for a tomorrow with less distress and more eustress.

In Part 4 you will be introduced to the Leverage Activation System™ (LAS), a simple and elegant way to infuse automicity into your daily life. Automicity will facilitate a hypnotic path of least resistance by building trust-based communication between your conscious and subconscious.

You will start to discover influences that used to faze you and cause distress will start to take care of themselves. Beneath the illusions that create confusion and conflict, what will become self-evident is that you are starting to replace working hard with working smart. This will include spending less energy cleaning up after the fallout of poorly made past decisions.

Summary

- **Coherence**, the measurement of the alignment of the conscious and subconscious mind.

- **Levnosis Attitudes**, this combination of hypnosis (and de-hypnosis) ideas aims to help us use leverage to align our conscious wants and subconscious habits.

- **What Works**, a linguistic dynamic aimed at gently tapping into the subconscious mind.

- **Fractionation**, a combination of dynamics that assist with **re-enforcement**.

- **Defractionation**, a combination of dynamics that assist with **re-evaluation**.

- **Automicity** creates natural pauses in our thinking and those pauses give a measure of control over the daily habits that we aim to improve for the better.

- **Autopilot and automicity** are both useful in our daily lives. Automicity is great for helping us improve the way we learn from our valuable life experiences.

In the next chapter we will look at how to transform automicity from a skill into a habit which will naturally bring more coherence and eustress into your life.

> Successful people are simply those with successful habits.

BRIAN TRACY

Aim Provide a way to make incremental changes that the subconscious will gladly accept because the changes align with its true nature.

Concepts
1 The Flinch Response.

2 Tapping into what already works for you.

Chapter 2.3

Harnessing Habits

I once saw a video of a US self-defence expert who mostly works with the police who face so many dangers and life-threatening situations. He explained that people operate on many levels; one of these is that primitive aspect which comes into play when we deal with unexpected danger. He labelled this the 'flinch response' and showed it in action in a very simple way. As he stood in front of a class of trainees and talked about it, now and then he'd sip water from a paper cup. Mid-sentence, as he looked directly forward, he threw the cup at someone out of his eye line to the side of him. The trainee instinctively threw up his arms to protect himself. The cup was actually empty but of course the trainee did not know that. He wasn't aware that he was being filmed either.

When the footage of the incident was slowed down, the expert pointed out how the trainee had thrown up both arms almost in the shape of a shield. This was a purely subconscious response. The instructor went on to explain that it is the first two to three seconds in real-life responses where the police - and any other professional in that situation - will often have difficulties. It's as if all the training they'd received conflicts with their natural primitive response. So the instructor showed the volunteer how to work with both and so remove the conflict. First he showed him how to become more conscious of the way he wanted to protect himself; then they built on that so it worked with his formal training rather than against it. As a result, in those first, crucial two to three seconds, the students were now able to combine their natural instinct with their structured training.

Many studies have tested the best self-defence methods for women, including everything from a strategically placed kick between the attacker's legs to gouging the attacker's eyes, using pepper spray, and even a high-heeled shoe as a hand weapon. The best overall response surprised me. It was found that shouting 'fire!' as loudly as possible would get the woman out of an attack more efficiently than any other method. The emergency responses from the public and safety services were measurably more effective. There was a list of reasons for this, such as members of the public preferring not to potentially associate or endanger themselves in a physical attack situation but much more willing to report a fire.

But there was also another reason. Attackers are mainly scared of one thing: attacking someone who is clearly more crazy than they are. A woman screaming 'fire' would be enough for the attacker to see that their plan, which is always very well-scripted and rehearsed in their mind, is no longer reliable. This is the element of surprise at its best.

These two examples show that behaviour in dangerous situations can be gauged on a spectrum with one side being natural and instinctive reactions and the other being trained responses. We can have:

- Instinctive reactions which sit on the 'natural' side of the spectrum, such as the flinch response. They come naturally to us so they should be easier for us to integrate.
- Trained responses that sit on the other side of the spectrum, such as the shouting 'fire!' example. These will be less easy for us to integrate naturally.

We will come back to the spectrum of natural responsiveness and how we can use both ends of it in our quest to harness our habits and make them work for us.

Why Such A Focus On Habits?

It is estimated that our habits make up 90% of our day and are the invisible architecture (structure and process) of daily life.

They align with the elusive obvious as even though we can recognise good habits from bad, beneficial from detrimental, they still keep a hold over us that is almost hypnotic. We seem to suspend the understanding that our habits shape our existence and our future for the security of the well-trodden path even if that is less than fulfilling.

We all have the ability to imagine and dream of a better life but as much as we lust after shiny objects and abilities that would set us apart and make us feel special, we still have an enormously hard time changing our habits, at least that is, the meaningful ones.

We know there are people who are highly adaptable; they're able to prioritise with ease and apply themselves to achieving what they want with little distraction. So what is it that separates people who can adopt or drop habits overnight from those who can't?

I believe there is another way of thinking about habits that might help us gain a new perspective on them so that we're able to wake up from the trance they've put us in. It'll offer a window of opportunity to transform the habits that don't work well for us.

Harness:
1. To put a harness on (a horse, donkey, dog, etc.); attach by a harness, as to a vehicle.
2. To bring under conditions for effective use; gain control over for a particular end. E.g. *to harness water power; to harness the energy of the sun.*

Habits:
1. An acquired behaviour pattern regularly followed until it has become almost involuntary. E.g. *the habit of looking both ways before crossing the street.*
2. Customary practice or use. E.g. *daily bathing is an American habit.*
3. A particular practice, custom, or usage. E.g. *the habit of shaking hands.*
4. A dominant or regular disposition or tendency; prevailing character or quality. E.g. *She has a habit of looking at the bright side of things.*
5. Addiction, especially to narcotics.
6. Mental character or disposition. E.g. *a habit of mind.*

(Taken from Dictionary.com)

We can take the meanings of each word, and combine and reorganise them into a useful new perspective:

Harness + Habits

= 'bring under conditions for effective use' + 'already acquired behaviour pattern'

= tapping into + what works for you already.

The aim is to work towards filling your day as much as possible with what works for you so that habits which don't work for you naturally and gradually drop away.

> We are attracted to the familiar but notice what is different.

This quote from the world of hypnosis is a fulcrum point that can ease us out of an old way of thinking and into a new one, which means we'd be acting on Einstein's advice. In a way it represents a conflict as the following example shows.

Advertisers have one goal: to influence you into buying something and allow an exchange to occur. This is usually money in exchange for making something in your life feel better. Before that happens they have to convince you that you are missing something, they need to create a conflict in your mind and then offer a solution. So the advertiser creates a new problem for you and kindly offers a solution, which, if they've done a good job, you will buy because they've also convinced you that they're trustworthy and worth listening to. Your subconscious mind sees this advertiser as an authority.

This subject alone could make for a whole book but I will just share one example. Arguably one of the most successful advertising campaigns was the one for the George Foreman Grill, which has sold more than one million and personally made George $200 million. When George added the tagline 'it's so good I put my name on it!' this was a great example of the application of 'we are attracted to the familiar but notice what is different'.

Attracted to the familiar: George was a world champion boxer who was able to compete at an age when most boxers could not survive the demands of the heavyweight division. His Lean Mean Fat-Reducing Grilling Machine aligned perfectly with his image. Out of the ring, he was well respected as a very religious man and a pillar of the community. The right celebrity has a well-known effect in advertising; the target audience subconsciously transfers its trust in the personality to the product advertised. And trust turns products into bestsellers time and time again.

Noticed what was different: At that time most sportspeople were promoting cars. Their influence drove (forgive the pun) the sales of motor vehicles. It was not the done thing for a sportsperson to link themselves with a grill for the home and initially George pushed back against the idea.

At this stage, you might be wondering what on earth boxers and grills have to do with harnessing habits. Hold your horses.... we will saddle up the subconscious as soon as we understand that if it can sell over a million grills then the hypnotic effect can surely help us update our habits.

We want to consciously sell our subconscious mind on the benefits of a change in habits so that it will buy into giving us a window of opportunity. This is not a zillion miles away from the money back guarantee that advertisers use. Our subconscious mind thinks that:

- Because they are kind enough to tell us a about a problem we didn't even know we had...
- Also, by chance, they happen to have a solution (at what is usually a bargain price)...
- And then they front the product with a personality who we would trust with our valuables...

   ...there is no way they'd try to sell us something really bad if they believed in the product so much that they would let us try it and then bring it back if it didn't delight us.

Would they?

Just to make it clear before moving on, I am not have a dig at the advertising industry as they often don't see that when they use persuasion techniques on the vulnerable masses they are affecting their own minds too. They mistakenly think that they are protected from their own selling techniques.

And if George genuinely believed his grill would benefit the health of the people purchasing it, then good on him!

Saddle Up A Trojan Horse

The Trojan horse first appeared in Homer's *Iliad*; it was the subterfuge the Greeks used to secretly enter the heavily fortified city of Troy and subsequently win the war. In computing, a Trojan Horse or Trojan is a program which misrepresents itself to appear useful, routine, or interesting in order to persuade a victim to install it.

You can see that the Trojan horse idea has a somewhat negative connotation, but I'd like to offer another point of view so please bear with me while I go on a bit of a diversion.

In Chapter 0.3, we had our first look at instant gratification and how it's a great example of misalignment between the conscious and subconscious. We learned from the Stanford University experiments that trust is essential if you want to develop delayed gratification. If trust is broken, this naturally drives you into a confused state and eventually towards immediate gratification.

Monty Roberts, known worldwide as 'The Horse Whisperer', brings together delayed gratification and our equestrian four-legged friend. I first learned of him when he appeared on the UK news showing his method for 'starting' horses rather than the old one of 'breaking' them. Her Majesty Queen Elizabeth was fascinated by his demonstration.

If you ever witness the traditional breaking method for horses, you may feel anything from surprised to traumatised because it uses so much effort and force to break the horse's will. When you understand how strong horses are - think horsepower - this method makes sense, but it's not a pleasant sight.

> Monty wanted his relationships to be built on trust and respect... it began with him simply observing how horses related to each other in their natural habitat.

Monty believed that the traditional breaking method was cruel and having witnessed it repeatedly as a child, he dedicated his life to finding another way.

It is worth noting that Monty had a very difficult relationship with his father, partly because of this adversarial approach to horses. His father came from a line of men where fear was more important than respect. In addition, discipline was taught through physical beatings and Monty endured many as he grew up in the hands of a man whose unpredictable rage was often fuelled by alcohol.

The one positive thing to come out of this dysfunctional relationship was Monty's determination to come up with an alternative to the usual breaking method.

In his autobiography, *The Man Who Listens to Horses*, Monty gives many examples of his father's tendency towards brutality and terror with horses and people once he was away from the eyes of the public. On one occasion Monty was chain whipped by his father.

Monty wanted his relationships to be built on trust and respect. As you might imagine, for a seven-year-old who had never experienced anything but brutality, he had his work cut out. This search began with Monty simply observing how horses related to each other in their natural habitat.

He observed the dynamics of how they communicated with each other, which with time gave him insights into the subtleties of both their verbal and non-verbal communication. We know that approximately 93% of all human communication is non-verbal; it seems that the horse world is no different. One of Monty's ideas was that the horse itself could do no wrong during his 'starting' process. This did two things:

- It took away the need for blame and punishment.
- He understood that if the horse didn't respond in a way that was useful then it was his communication that needed to change.

Through patient trial and error, he eventually created a system that brought the horse to his side with a saddle on its back in just 20 minutes. This was done with no pain or force. He systematically showed the horse that he wanted to be friends. He was speaking the horse's own language and the horse could relate to him as a trusted leader of the herd. This meant that the 'breaking' method, which usually took days or even weeks, started to lose its hold on the equestrian community.

Monty's father did not give any credit or respect to his son for his accomplishment and their relationship never healed. But although Monty couldn't heal his relationship with his father, he was able to change the history of violence within his family.

He rolled out his ideas to whoever was interested. As you might imagine, traditionalists were very nervous of his new ways but even traditionalists are businessmen and if starting only took minutes whereas breaking usually took days, then it didn't make sense to stick to the old method.

Monty went on to marry and have three children and his understanding of communication was to pay huge dividends. He and his wife took in many children from troubled families where abuse and violence was common. Over the years, 47 children were able to live in a home where patience, trust, respect and love were not just spoken of; they were practiced every single day. Monty called it 'tough love' where discipline was applied appropriately, proportionately and consistently as a method for creating healthy, happy people.

Scientists and psychologists visited Monty to find out what he was doing and what they could learn from a man who could turn a wild horse into a friend in minutes. So Monty began to speak and teach. He was nicknamed 'The Horse Whisperer' because he never ever needed to raise his voice when starting a horse. As mentioned earlier, one career pinnacle was the demonstration for Queen Elizabeth II at Windsor Castle in England. Being a world-renowned horse owner and enthusiast, her royal seal of approval was a message that travelled the world. There was no turning back for the starting system as more and more people wanted to witness it.

I'm focusing on Monty because of his success with 'tough love'. He and his wife instilled trust and love in youngsters who had experienced confusion and mixed messages in their most formative years from adults who had probably experienced the same mixed messages too.

Tough love is basically about setting healthy boundaries; it also develops discernment so that we can separate truth from fiction. With tough love:

1. There is no punishment. The drama is removed from situations and a common sense attitude takes its place. The enjoyment and satisfaction that comes from activities, which often teach delayed gratification, remains.
2. The adult keeps their own hurts and disappointments out of tense situations. They don't act from them, instead they're aware of them and they deal with them; they have healthy boundaries and act as a role model.
3. Boundaries are consistent and based on compassion.
4. Boundaries, though consistent, can still adapt to life's changes.
5. Delayed gratification is inherent within it. This leads to children developing healthy reward systems and they learn the difference between reacting and responding to life.

We want to have a 'starting' relationship with our own mind rather than a 'breaking' relationship.

Now let's go back to habits. The best habits are the ones that are easy, simple, take very little time yet give us something valuable, such as cleaning your teeth.

Starting Habits

Most people have a dominant side; statistics show that anywhere between 70-95% of people are right-handed. We often do things with our dominant side, such as brushing our teeth, as we tend to go through our daily routine on autopilot. Most of us use our dominant hand to brush our teeth even though dentists tell us that using only one hand leads to some teeth not getting a good brushing. Ideally you'd use both hands to brush your teeth, splitting the time in half. Of course, using the non-dominant hand feels very strange until it becomes a habit. This is simply because our non-dominant hand and arm are not used to holding and using the brush.

Let's tap into this existing habit of brushing our teeth with our dominant hand as a way of integrating a new habit. I've found it to be very effective. However, it's just an example and you could try something else if you prefer, such as learning to write with your other hand.

Brushing your teeth with your non-dominant hand, although it feels odd at first, is high in its level of naturalness (like the flinch response) and is fairly easy to integrate - with a little patience. A friend of mine from my school days, who broke his right collarbone playing as a goalkeeper in a football match, jokingly told me how quickly he learned to use his other hand for his daily ablutions. When we transfer a skill from the dominant to the non-dominant side, the mind takes what it already knows and adapts more quickly.

Automicity is far less natural to us (see Chapter 2.2) and so it is much trickier to integrate, such as a woman shouting 'fire' rather than automatically panicking during an attack. This is because we are creating an interruption to the mind.

Harnessing A New Habit

In Part 4 we'll bring together aspects of Parts 1, 2 and 3. For now, we'll gain some experience with harnessing habits. It's up to you which existing habit you'd like to experiment with. Be mindful that this is about experiencing the process rather than attaining a specific outcome.

Between now and the time you get to Part 4 and go through the experiences there, I want you to get a feel for linking an existing habit with a new habit. What follows is a new daily activity for you to do - one which could potentially become a great habit for the rest of your life.

EXPERIENCE 7: SADDLE UP YOUR TROJAN HORSE

For most people, brushing their teeth is a morning and night-time activity. Select one of these times.

- Brush your teeth with your dominant hand for half the time you usually spend on this task.

- Switch hands to your non-dominant hand and brush for the same amount of time. So it's half one hand and then half the other.

- Please do this at least three days in a row.

If you have great dexterity, go ahead with the usual horizontal and vertical brushing movements. If you struggle a bit, don't be fazed. The up and down vertical movements are very tricky so just stick with the horizontal movements to get the initial benefit of the experience.

Whichever motion you use, it will feel totally unnatural to begin with, but that feeling fades naturally with repetition and persistence. If you continued with this exercise you'd eventually discover that your mind/body connection soon transfers what it knows from your dominant side to your non-dominant side. You will probably never get quite as good with your non-dominant hand but you will get very close over time.

The Experience 7 exercise shows us how to install a good programme into our subconscious mind without its defences being engaged, just like the Trojan horse in fact. We are slipping the skill of de-fractionation under the radar with the change from the dominant to non-dominant side.

Further on, we will harness our teeth brushing habit (or another one of your daily habits of your choice) so that it becomes a reminder to engage automicity every day. This will help you maximise what you have learned that day.

> As you bring your consciousness to bear on how you create one very specific habit, this will bring you a measure of control over **all** of your habits.

There is also a tough love element in that although our habitual nature will push back against using the non-dominant hand there is a useful and practical reason for doing so in terms of improving oral health. Ask a dental hygienist - they'll tell you that there are parts of the mouth which get less attention when we only brush with one hand. Brushing with both hands, although not comfortable to begin with, will be beneficial for you in the long term if you make it a habit.

The aim of Experience 7 is to give us a flavour of de-fractionation and also what it takes to become ambidextrous where it can be very useful. More importantly however, it is to help you see that this is the way you have developed all your good (and bad) habits: you have linked one thing with another. As you bring your consciousness to bear on how you create one very specific habit, this will bring you a measure of control over **all** of your habits. We'll cover this in more depth in Part 4.

Summary

- There are more natural and less natural ways for tapping into our habits. Both are valid and there are ways to integrate them as a combination to make for even more leverage and to make automicity a vital habit.

- New habits can be linked to other existing habits. This is applying Natural Learning.

- Harnessing habits is about filling as much as our day as possible with what works for us.

In the next chapter we will look at how to develop a practice mindset...

Recapitulation of Terms

What works for me - Things that make up your day that create a better quality of life.

What doesn't work for me - Things that make up your day that create a lower quality of life.

Fractionation - The way the mind naturally works by association; it glues things together and makes meaning as a person learns. This can be considered as a form of hypnosis.

Defractionation - The way the mind unglues naturally (but not obviously) which opens up space for new learnings. This can be considered as a form of de-hypnosis.

Autopilot - The time during which the mind is running 100% on its habitual nature.

Automicity - The act of applying intent to take the mind off autopilot for just enough time to take a measure of control over our habitual nature.

Part 3

The Purposeful Practice Filter (Momentum Leverage)

> An ounce of practice is worth more than tons of preaching.
>
> MAHATMA GANDHI

> "Practice is everything."

PERIANDER

Aim To make it absolutely clear that you are always practicing, whether you know it or not, whether you admit it or not. This will help you become more selective with how you spend the time that makes up your present day.

Concepts 1 Daoist habitual model.

2 Effective practice formula.

Chapter 3.1

You become what you practice

In Part 2, we focused on how we can use automicity to take a measure of control over our autopilot and how to use defractionation and its pausing effect to gain some insight into what we usually do without a second thought. Now it's time to move things up a gear.

The Daoist Perspective On Practice

In Daoism there is a huge emphasis on the nature of what we would call causality. Figure 7 below is split into Past, Present and Future with all three aspects summed up by 'you are a combination of all your habits'. The truth is that human nature is really human habit.

We learn new things and these are like software updates on our computers. Our automatic pilot uses them to make incremental changes to how we react and respond to life.

The police often wonder if witnesses have seen the same event because their statements vary so much. We all delete, distort and generalise through the perceptual filter mechanism that we looked at earlier. So bear this in mind as you consider **you are what you remember** - although we cannot change the past, we can change how we remember it in our minds.

You might already have noticed that at the end of each Part, there is a Recapitulation section. There are also summaries at the end of each chapter but their intent is slightly different. The recaps are more about punctuating and gradually building on the conceptual elements of the book as it progresses. We are building concepts on concepts in a way that aligns with Natural Learning.

You get what you rehearsed may sound obvious (remember the elusive obvious?) but it is muscle memory that gets us through each day including this present day as you are reading these words.

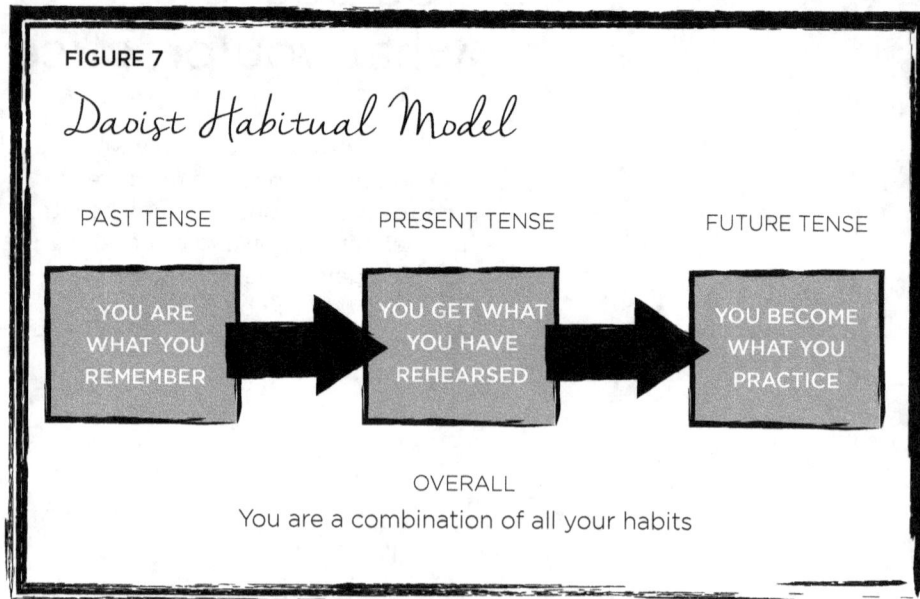

When people begin to work on any form of self-development, they tend to focus more on the future and the idea that they can shape the person they will become. Sadly, many lose their faith in their ability to shape their future as they have lacked consistent results in the past. However, if you are doing the exercises in this book, you've experienced automicity and so have more than just an intellectual idea about what purposeful practice truly is. This will become clearer as we progress.

Meaning And Origin

When you ask people what practice means for them, the usual answers range from practicing a musical instrument for a recital, practicing a sport for an event or practicing something that's memory-based such as a child learning their seven times table.

Before we discuss practice in detail, let's look at the meaning and origin of the word. (Definitions are taken from Dictionary.com)

Practice:
1. Habitual or customary performance; operation: office practice. Habit; custom: *It is not the practice here for men to wear long hair.*
2. Repeated performance or systematic exercise for the purpose of acquiring skill or proficiency. E.g. *Practice makes perfect.*
3. Condition arrived at by experience or exercise. E.g. *She refused to play the piano because she was out of practice.*
4. The action or process of performing or doing something. E.g. *To put a scheme into practice.*
5. The exercise or pursuit of a profession or occupation, especially law or medicine. E.g. *She plans to set up practice in her hometown.*
6. The business of a professional person. E.g. *The doctor wanted his daughter to take over his practice when he retired.*

Origin: A derivative of *prāctica* meaning, practical work.

So 'practice' derives from prāctica which means practical work. Bear that in mind as you look at number three in the list from the dictionary.

Practice = repeated performance or systematic exercise for the purpose of acquiring *practical* skill or proficiency.

The reason I emphasise the practical element is that, as much as possible, we want to develop an insight into **how** problems occur. I've emphasised how for good reason. When we focus on 'why' it doesn't get us very far. 'Why' makes us look backwards and we do our best to fill in the parts we left out when we deleted, distorted and generalised. The best we can do is guess. However, if we have very reliable sources to help us fill in the gaps then asking 'why' may be useful to a degree.

When we ask 'how' we tap into the idea that problems are rarely based on one-off events. We usually find that a problem is something that has compounded and accumulated to a point where we can no longer ignore it.

As we become more skilled in practicing things that help us have more of what works for us in our lives, we will slowly gain more insight into the 'you become what you practice' dynamic.

Effective Practice Formula

We can break practice down into two key elements:

Effective Practice = Deliberate Practice + Systematic Practice

= (consciously and intentionally) + (applied according to a fixed plan or system; methodical)

Have you noticed that a pattern is beginning to emerge? In Part 1, we split stress into distress and eustress to help us untangle our minds. In Part 2, we built on eustress with 'What Works for You', and distress with 'What Doesn't Work for You'. Now, by splitting practice into deliberate practice and systematic practice, we are once again working with Daoist principles, the separation part of the separate and combine concept.

Deliberate practice
With deliberate practice not only would you, for example, follow the instructions given in Part 2, you would also break down the ideas into specific parts, research and work on one element until you've made some improvement and only then move on to the next one. Deliberate practice is a skill that takes time to develop.

For example, university was a big change for me as up to that time teachers had always supplied me with everything I needed to study and pass exams. This wasn't the case at university. Here lectures only outlined a subject - it was up to me to do the in-depth research. There was no way I'd pass my exams if I just attended the lectures. This was a steep learning curve but one that stood me in good stead for later life when I became a chartered engineer. I got paid to solve problems and get paid better when I do it more efficiently and effectively than the next guy or gal.

In Chapter 3.2 we will look at deliberate practice from a leverage mindset to help wire this into your psyche.

Systematic practice
In Part 2 we looked at how we can make a daily practice by linking a new habit to an existing one. In this case, we created a new habit which is so doable that it's difficult for the subconscious mind to stop us from testing it out for a period

of time. We created a new neural pathway just by brushing our teeth with our non-dominant hand - and at the same time we experienced automicity in action. I've continued to brush my teeth with both hands and as the days, weeks, months and years passed, I've created a habit that gives me huge value for very little effort.

In Chapter 3.3 we will look in greater depth at systematic practice from a leverage mindset.

A Practice Mindset Role Model

When I hear the word practice I immediately think of the South African professional golfer Gary Player who is arguably the most successful golfer of all time, on and off the course. His impeccable set of values, stringent health and fitness regime, and insistence on quality, have earned him admiration the world over. His merits and achievements include:

- Winning the British Open aged 23 and the 1965 U.S. Open at the age of 29.
- In 1965, he became the only non-American to win all four majors making up the Grand Slam.
- His rating as the world's eighth greatest golfer by Golf Digest magazine in 2000, some 35 years after his finest year.
- Being named South African Sportsman of the Century in 2000.
- Posing nude in ESPN's The Magazine Annual Body Issue in July 2013. Quite a feat for a 77-year-old!
- Winning 165 tournaments over five decades.
- Designing 325 golf courses around the world.
- Setting up the Gary Player Stud Farm which has received worldwide acclaim for breeding more than 2,000 top thoroughbred racehorses.
- Establishing the Player Foundation in 1983 to support less fortunate children living in rural areas of South Africa. The Foundation has raised more than $50 million.
- Building the Blair Atholl Schools in Johannesburg, South Africa through the Player Foundation. The schools have educated more than 500 students from kindergarten through to grade eight.

In an interview in Golf Digest magazine in 2002 Player said: "I was practicing in a bunker down in Texas and this good old boy with a big hat stopped to watch. The first shot he saw me hit went in the hole. He said, 'You got 50 bucks if you knock the next one in.' I holed the next one. Then he says, 'You got $100 if you hole the next one.' In it went for three in a row. As he peeled off the bills he said, 'Boy, I've never seen anyone so lucky in my life. And I responded back, 'Well, the harder I practice... the luckier I get."

Maybe it is no coincidence that every great sports star has a similar story to share: they make their own luck by going the extra mile in terms of practice while others hold back. This is especially true of the ones who are misleadingly called 'naturals'.

Seeing Serendipity Everywhere

Professor Richard Wiseman's *The Luck Factor* contains a decade of learning from his base at the University of Hertfordshire. He researched people's perceptions about their own luck and rated these people on an extrovert/introvert scale. He discovered that people who scored high for extroversion were most likely to describe themselves as 'lucky'. He also discovered that, because of their extrovert personality, these people naturally had more fortuitous encounters. Their openness and friendliness meant that they were less susceptible to negative emotional states and even illness.

Wiseman designed experiments that created the same opportunities for people to experience luck or chance. The people involved in the study were a mixture; some clearly saw themselves as 'lucky' while others considered themselves 'unlucky'.

One of these interventions strategically placed some money on a coffee shop floor near a businessman who was also part of the experiment. Two people, one who felt herself to be unlucky and the other who thought things always worked out well for him and was naturally lucky, were introduced into the scenario. The lucky guy immediately noticed the money on the ground, pocketed it, and then struck up a conversation with the businessman. The 'unlucky' woman meanwhile, looked directly ahead, stepped right over the cash and sipped her coffee without saying a word.

Although I like Wiseman's work as it suggests that we have a measure of control over our luck, I would like him to expand on how introverts can create the conditions to experience better luck without having to change their personality.

The following definition of luck matches how most people think of it:

Luck: That which happens to a person; an event, good or ill, affecting one's interests or happiness, and which is deemed casual; a course or series of such events regarded as occurring by chance; chance; hap; fate; fortune; often, one's habitual or characteristic fortune; as, good, bad, ill, or hard luck. Luck is often used for good luck; as, luck is better than skill.

The 'luck is better than skill' part makes me feel more than a little uncomfortable as I think it would help someone give up, telling themselves that they are at the mercy of chance and circumstance. Of course there are things in life that we cannot change however there are also many things we can - and this includes the attitude towards the things we cannot change.

I prefer to think of luck as the skill of increasing the potential of being in the right place at the right time. I also like the following as a quote:

 Luck is when opportunity meets preparation.

SENECA

As this book is focused on leverage, you can understand how my RAS is looking for fulcrum points wherever they may be hiding. Could it be that luck is a fulcrum point? That sweet spot that falls between all our preparations for life and the times when our RAS is awake enough to see the opportunities that are always around us? Just a thought!

From this point of view we understand that luck isn't something that just happens to us. Serendipity is anything but luck; it realises the basic nature of how things work and then works on aligning with them.

I believe that automicity as a practice works at washing away the underlying resistance that might hold someone back from making adequate preparation and from honing in on opportunities. By tapping into what works for us already, it is aiming to align us with our own source of luck - coherence.

The practice of automicity is not about getting anything for free. There wouldn't be any satisfaction otherwise. It takes effort not because it is difficult but because it is so simple and subtle, and therefore so easy to dismiss in terms of its amazing effectiveness.

We can see that the more skilled you get at automicity, the more serendipity and synchronicity you will naturally invite into your life because you will have genuinely earned it.

Summary

- Most people are not aware of what they are practicing. The subconscious sees the way we spend this day as practice for what we want more of tomorrow and beyond.

- Practicing both systematically and deliberately not only makes practice more effective - together they can create great leverage.

- When we find practices that align with what works for us already, our luck naturally improves.

In the next chapter we'll build on the deliberate practice idea by looking at the power of compounding, which can be our friend or foe.

> Albert Einstein, when asked what he considered to be the most powerful force in the universe, answered: 'Compound interest!' What you have become is the price you paid to get what you used to want.

MIGNON MCLAUGHLIN

Aim Tap into the power of compound interest to support effective practice and so bring about increased coherence.

Concepts 1 Compound Interest.

2 Deliberate practice.

Chapter 3.2

Compounding By Design

In my role as a Chartered Design Engineer, I have had to work with certain rules around how we interface our wants and desires with the laws of nature. For example, gravity is one law that we are wise to respect. Every time we fly on a plane we benefit from the Bernoulli principle, the physics that explains how the shape of an aeroplane's wings allows it to leave terra firma. As with gravity, time is also fixed yet we can work with it to make it work for us or work against us.

Problems rarely appear out of the blue and once one appears more tend to follow. Sometimes it feels like an avalanche where only a small section of snow moves then, because of gravity, the weight shifts more snow and in a very short space of time, it all comes crashing down.

Daoists look beyond immediate causes to earlier stages of a change or event; they call it 'one step earlier'. I experienced this when I had a treatment for a shoulder problem. The acupressure specialist said that it was my neck area that was the actual issue. I didn't believe it until she worked on my neck and then down my whole spine working gently on the trigger points to bring everything back into natural alignment. Within two days, my shoulder had returned to normal. After a number of follow-up visits over the following year, the treatments worked quicker and lasted longer. The problematic shoulder pain helped me discover the real problem - my spinal alignment was not good enough to support high-level Kung Fu training. If I had opted instead for the more traditional physiotherapy for my shoulder, I would probably not have discovered the underlying cause. This is a tricky aspect of life in the West. We are so entrained into immediate gratification that we naturally tend to look for the magic pill to make the pain go away quickly rather than looking for the causal factor.

Once again we are going to follow Einstein's advice and move beyond the same thinking that created our problems. First we'll look at how things either grow into problems that are bad for us or solutions that are good for us.

> Always do your best. What you plant now, you will harvest later.
>
> OG MANDINO

Compound Interest

The old saying 'you reap what you sow' is usually intoned in the voice of doom, often to someone who is experiencing negative consequences from previous actions. However Mandino's quote points out that if we always do our best then we'll reap those dividends too. It all goes back to delayed gratification.

The way the subconscious mind naturally learns is akin to a savings account where time brings compounded interest.

George Samuel Clason's *The Richest Man in Babylon* dispenses financial advice through a collection of parables set in ancient Babylon. Through their experiences in business and managing household accounts, the characters in the stories learn simple lessons in financial wisdom. The parables are aimed at setting financial goals not only to advance in one's career or position, but also to become wiser and more knowledgeable. This includes having compassion for those less fortunate and helping them within reasonable limits.

One of the teachings from Clason's classic is the idea that once you've started saving at least one-tenth of what you earn, you must put that money to work earning interest. The figure used was 10% so that the aim was to live off the remaining 90% of your earnings. You may initially think that 10% isn't much and you could be right. What we see however is that the dynamic of interest being compounded over time is not linear.

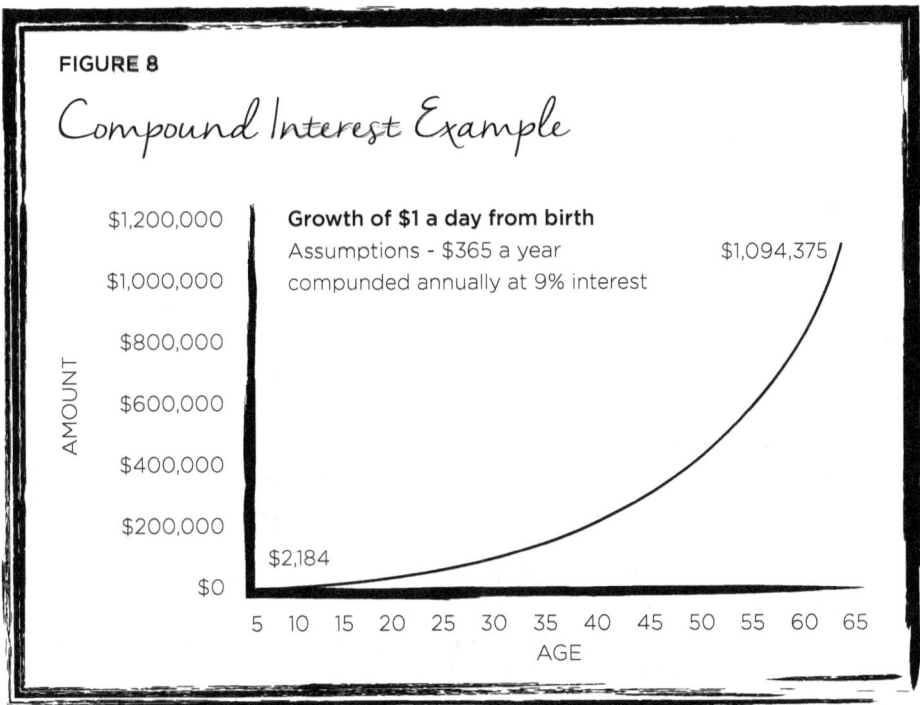

FIGURE 8

Compound Interest Example

Growth of $1 a day from birth
Assumptions - $365 a year compounded annually at 9% interest

This example graph applies a 9% interest rate which could be considered as too high especially as interest rates have averaged approximately 5% over the past century. However there are a number of factors that are useful to observe:

1. Interest rates are always dependant on the risk you are willing to take.
If you think that investing in the stock market is completely different from gambling in a casino, you need to understand that the statistical analysis methods that both apply are identical. Gambling only differs from investment because its finish line is dictated from the outset. Of course, I don't advise that you bet your shirt on a horse rather than investing in a fund or bank. It's best if you match the level of risk you take on with your overall outlook on

life; so if you're a cautious person you will feel safer with a more conservative investment strategy.

Below, we can see an example of just how much percentage growth can vary depending on the level of risk a person is willing to take. The example shows a range of 1.53% for low-risk guaranteed growth all the way up to 58.2% for a high-risk technology that could turn into a loss in a heartbeat.

Average ISA Performance During 2014/15 Tax Year
(Source: Investment Life & Pensions Moneyfacts/Lipper)

2014/15 Tax Year	% Growth
Average Cash ISA	1.53%
Average Stocks & Shares ISA	7.4%
Best Performing Stocks & Shares ISA Fund Sector	18.9% (North America)
Best Performing Stocks & Shares ISA Fund	58.2% (AXA Framlington Biotech Fund)

2. Time is the key factor.
The illustration shows compound interest at work. It demonstrates that saving only $1 a day from birth would allow someone to retire as a millionaire.

It might be worth considering that being a millionaire is not most people's true desire. The true attraction is the freedom of choice to do what they want with their time which is what they associate with the millionaire status. The following story is often used by trainers and motivational speakers.[1]

> An American businessman was standing at the pier of a coastal Mexican village when a small boat with just one fisherman docked. Inside the boat were several large yellow fin tuna. The American complimented the Mexican on the quality of his fish.
>
> "How long did it take you to catch them?" the American asked.
>
> "Only a little while," the Mexican replied.
>
> "Why don't you stay out longer and catch more fish?"

---
[1] I found this version at: http://www.digitalsparkmarketing.com/inspirational-stories/measuring-success

"I have enough to support my family's immediate needs."

"But what do you do with the rest of your time?"

The Mexican fisherman said: "I sleep late, fish a little, play with my children, take a siesta with my wife, Maria, stroll into the village each evening where I sip wine and play guitar with my amigos. I have a full and busy life, senor."

The American scoffed: "I am a Harvard MBA and could help you. You should spend more time fishing and with the proceeds you could buy a bigger boat and, with the proceeds from the bigger boat, you could buy several boats. Eventually you would have a fleet of fishing boats. Instead of selling your catch to a middleman, you would sell directly to the consumers, eventually opening your own canning factory. You would control the product, processing and distribution. You would need to leave this small coastal fishing village and move to Mexico City, then LA and eventually NYC where you will run your expanding enterprise."

"But senor, how long will this all take?"

"Fifteen to twenty years."

"But what then, senor?"

The American laughed: "That's the best part. When the time is right, you would announce an IPO - an Initial Public Offering - and sell your company stock to the public and become very rich. You would make millions!"

"Millions, senor? Then what?"

"Then you would retire. Move to a small fishing village where you would sleep late, fish a little, play with your kids, take a siesta with your wife, stroll to the village in the evenings where you could sip wine and play your guitar with your amigos…"

Designing Your 'Dollar a Day'

The message I got from the Babylon parables was that we invest every day whether we are fully aware of it or not because time itself is the main compounder, which in turn emphasises the importance of mastering delayed gratification. With this in mind, my aim is that you become much more mindful of what you do each day as what you do today accurately predicts your future.

'Dollar a Day' is the term I use to remind myself that it's lots of little successes that bring benefits including increasing eustress. The fisherman's story helps me see that removing things that don't add real quality to my life helps too.

Summary

- A problem or a solution is only ever experienced when it is compounded enough to become noticeable to us.

- Compounding is not linear; it takes some time for the benefits to really accumulate. Sow now and reap later.

- Compound interest is a useful analogy because it helps us see that time is also one of our precious resources.

In the next chapter we will look at how something as simple as slumber can help us with systematic practice.

173

> Sleep is that golden chain that ties health and our bodies together.

THOMAS DEKKER

Aim — To apply awareness and compounding to an area that can be considered a fulcrum point for us all - high-quality rest leading to a deeply restful night's sleep.

Concepts

1 Reinvigoration Reminder.

2 Utilising REM.

3 Waking State Model.

Chapter 3.3

Even While You Sleep

Once upon a time, a farmer was approached by a fresh-faced enthusiastic young salesman with a litany of new products such as the latest agrochemicals and labour-saving devices. The salesman eulogised about how using a combination of the products could increase the farmer's yields anywhere between 5-20%. The farmer agreed that the figures were indeed impressive and said he appreciated the science that helped him and his fellow farmers save time and energy while growing more food for their customers.

He firstly shared with the young salesman how his grandfather, one in a long line of farmers, if offered the latest tractor and a shovel to sow a field would always choose the shovel. He'd enjoyed the satisfaction that comes from working hard doing something useful, eating his well-earned meal and then having a good night's sleep.

Then the farmer responded to the salesman how much he appreciated the products on offer, but went on to say that if he applied just 10% of what he already knew and owned to boost his yield, he would get more than a mere 20% improvement.

People generally underestimate the amount of wisdom they hold within. At least this farmer knew he wasn't making the most of what he had already experienced and learned.

Untapped Wisdom

I believe there is a very good reason why we don't tap into our own wisdom. In the last chapter, we saw that if we compound problems over time it will be difficult to balance their effect because things compound when they have not been addressed by the conscious mind. This is, in essence, long-term fatigue, a form of distress that affects our limbic system.

Most of us know the difference between a solid night's sleep and a disturbed night's sleep. Everyone wants to sleep well so they can be as refreshed as possible and balance out the daily fatigue which so easily compounds and creates problems out of things that wouldn't faze us if we were well rested.

It's important that we understand our own sleep patterns based on how we live our waking day. However, we will only ever get the true benefits when we also invest in the regular spring clean effects that we introduced in Part 2 and will delve into more in Part 4.

The prevailing attitude in most modern societies is all about working hard to earn the basic reward of rest and sleep. We know that when we work and exercise the body well (like the farmer in the story above), the quality of sleep improves. In terms of the mind body connection however, it seems that we might be wise to consider that the reverse is more useful. Rather than considering quality rest and sleep as being a reward, think of them as being the fundamental prerequisites for a mind that makes clear healthy decisions.

What if our work then was reliant on the eustress that comes from high-quality sleep? What if people were as mindful about their sleep as they were about their work? Would good quality rest and sleep allow them to follow Einstein's advice with ease so that they could shift their thinking when they needed to? Remember the quote: 'We cannot solve our problems with the same thinking we used when we created them.' This is the third time this quote has popped up and it might not be the last time either because it is so fundamental.

Reminder For Reinvigoration

Generally speaking, good sleep leads to better sleep and bad sleep leads to worse. Compounding on a series of good sleeps makes for more highly restful sleep as well as waking up feeling fresh and ready to go. You might say that is obvious. There is also a negative spiral to low-quality sleep when we wake feeling that we haven't had enough rest and it seems that we are playing catch up all day long. That's obvious too!

What is less obvious is that how we rest during our waking day helps create a good night's sleep. If we try to put all of our rest requirements into our sleep at night, we miss out on the benefits of sharing the rest and recuperation load throughout the whole 24-hour cycle.

> Insomnia is costing the average US worker 11.3 days or $2,280 in lost productivity every year...

Jon Kabat-Zinn is a meditation expert who works with many forward-thinking companies on how to use mindfulness meditation to improve the health of their employees. He cites the scientific support for meditation which shows there is a good business basis for assisting their employees as the well-being effects of meditation filter all the way through their working day. When Kabat-Zinn gave a presentation to Google, an employee raised a query on how she couldn't stay awake when meditating. She was quite advanced in the practice so was expecting a highly technical solution. There was a look of confusion on her face when she heard Jon's simple response. He said that she was most likely sleep deprived and that meditation was a great way to highlight this very common problem.

Most of us are sleep deprived but just have to manage with the fatigue the best we can. Too many of us accept it as normal.

However science is starting to catch onto lack of sleep such as the insomnia effect on the US workforce.

Insomnia is costing the average US worker 11.3 days or $2,280 in lost productivity every year, according to a study in the September 2011 issue of the journal SLEEP. "We were shocked by the enormous impact insomnia has on the average person's life," said lead author Ronald C. Kessler, Ph.D. "It's an under-appreciated problem. Americans are not missing work because of insomnia. They are still going to their jobs but accomplishing less because they're tired. In an information-based economy, it's difficult to find a condition that has a greater effect on productivity." The results were computed from a national sampling of 7,428 employees, part of the larger American Insomnia Study undertaken by Harvard Medical School.[2]

In a well-balanced life, the three main areas of a typical day are work, rest and play. If we assign eight hours to each of those three, you'll see that rest for most people is their eight-hour night-time sleep (if they are lucky). But you'd struggle to find an adult who plays for eight hours a day so perhaps we are not as well balanced as we think.

Through applying the concepts within this book backed up with tonnes of research and a willingness to test things out, I have discovered a simple model that works for me. I invite you to test these ideas for yourself if you feel that your energy levels don't meet your daily needs.

Four states are shown in Figure 9. We experience many states in every given day; I believe however that these four are where we can make incremental changes and improvements that will then automatically and naturally filter down into all the key areas of our lives. This includes health, relationships and finances.

These four levels of wakefulness include sleep itself which may raise an eyebrow… However, consider that even sleep is a form of wakefulness from the point of view of the subconscious mind. You might have been woken from a deep sleep by extreme weather or suspicious noises that sounded like an intruder in your home. People who have undergone surgery under anaesthetic have been known to say afterwards that they recall what was going on in the operating theatre even though they cannot explain how. Your subconscious is always aiming to protect you from danger so it's always switched on even when you may think you're unconscious.

---

[2] Source http://www.aasmnet.org/articles.aspx?id=2521

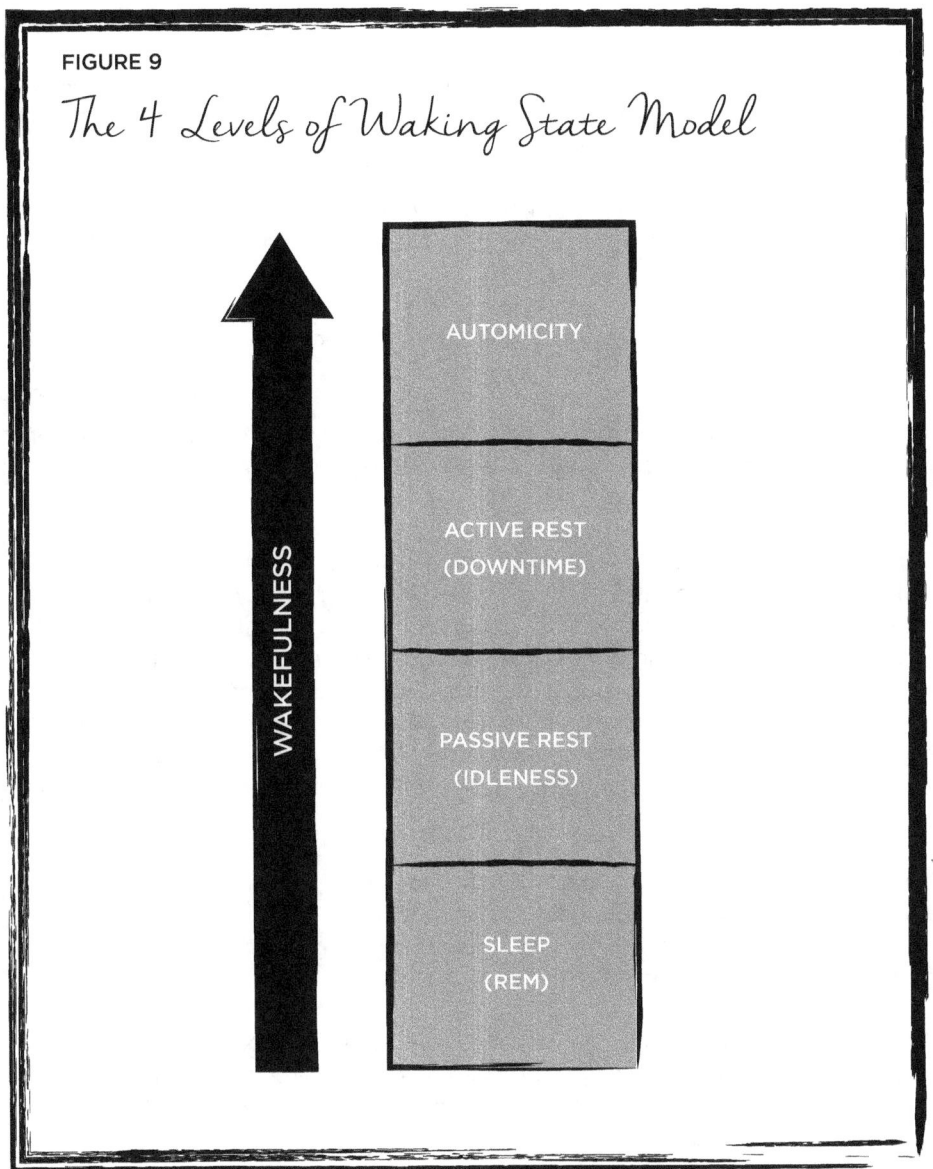

FIGURE 9

The 4 Levels of Waking State Model

The above shows a visual representation of the four states and you'll see that two of the four are based on rest. Cast your mind back to when we applied ideo dynamic leverage to divide stress into good stress and bad stress; we can now use this approach in a slightly different way. Rather than good and bad, we'll think in terms of active and passive. This divide is used extensively in Daoist martial arts as all physical movement follows this idea and so can help create fast and dynamic movements while still maintaining a relaxed manner that conserves energy.

Rest has been broken into two categories. The first is Idleness which can be thought of as passive rest. The second is Downtime which is rest that is more active in nature. People will differ as to what activities tick the box for active and passive rest. I'll share my own ideas as usual, but it will be up to you to test and find out what works for you personally.

The last of the four states is Automicity which we will look at in some more detail towards the end of this chapter as I believe it will help make the other three states blend together even better.

Let's look at each of these four primary states in their reverse order of wakefulness:

4. Sleep: To take the rest afforded by a suspension of voluntary bodily functions and the natural suspension, complete or partial, of consciousness; cease being awake. (From Dictionary.com)

Considering approximately a third of our life is spent in deep sleep, it is something that most of us don't know much about or really consider unless we are deprived of it for some time. Sleep studies have identified that we pass through five stages during our slumber. The first stage is a very light sleep from which it is easy to wake up. The second stage moves into a slightly deeper sleep, and stages three and four represent our deepest sleep. Our brain activity throughout these stages is gradually slowing down so that by the time we are deeply asleep, we experience nothing but delta which are the slowest brain waves.

The fifth stage, which is known as REM, has mystified mankind for generations and still does to this day. Rapid eye movement (REM) was first documented back in 1953 by University of Chicago researchers. It is primarily characterised by the active movements of the eyes.

The four stages outside of REM are called non-REM sleep (NREM). Although most dreams take place during REM, more recent research has shown that dreams can occur during any of the sleep stages; however they don't have the intensity of REM dreams.

We cycle through these five stages several times throughout a typical night's sleep. Each subsequent cycle, however, includes more REM sleep and less deep sleep (stages three and four). By morning, we're having almost all stage one, two and five (REM) sleep. It is believed that seven cycles of REM is generally what makes for a good night's sleep.

Researchers have investigated what happens if we don't get any REM sleep. The original theory was that no REM sleep meant no dreams and that dreams were a sort of safety valve that helped your brain let off steam that you couldn't let off during the day. Some studies showed that people who had their REM interrupted and were not able to dream became anxious, irritable and had difficulty concentrating.

> ...people who had their REM interrupted and were not able to dream became anxious, irritable and had difficulty concentrating.

Some of the latest ideas on REM and dreaming are associated with learning. This connection seems strong because infants and toddlers experience much more REM than adults. We also tend to sleep less in our later years when most adults don't see so much value in investing their efforts in continuing education.

One area of dreaming that raises researchers' curiosity is why we forget what we experience in our dreams so quickly upon waking. Freud theorised that we forget our dreams because they contain our repressed thoughts and wishes and so we wouldn't want to remember them anyway. L. Strumpell, a dream researcher from the same era as Freud, believed that several things contribute to it. For one, he said that many things are quickly forgotten when you first wake up, such as physical sensations. He also considered the fact that many dream images are not very intense and would therefore be easy to forget. Another reason, and probably the strongest of his theories, is that we traditionally learn and remember both by association and repetition and therefore only recall the dreams that repeat themselves.

So we can see that researchers think that REM is where we make meaning of our daily life and learn as much as we can from our experiences yet what we learn is somehow integrated very quickly and subtly such that when we wake, we are ready to get on with our day.

Deirdre Barrett, a psychologist at Harvard University, presented her theory at the 2010 Boston meeting of the Association of Psychological Science. She has found that our slumbering hours may help us solve puzzles that have plagued us during daylight hours.

Barrett's theory on dreaming boiled down to: dreaming is really just thinking, but in a slightly different state from when our eyes are open. "Whatever the state we're put in, we're still working on the same problems," she said.

Barrett conducted many studies over a 10 year period to test how REM and dreaming could be solving problems on our behalf. It gives some credence to the saying 'sleep on it' when a person has an important decision to make. In one study, Barrett had college students pick a simple homework problem to try to solve in a dream. The students focused on them each night before they went to bed. At the end of a week, about half the students had dreamed about the problem and about a quarter had experienced a dream which had contained the answer.

Barrett has also extensively reviewed scientific and historical literature looking for examples of problems solved in dreams. Einstein's theory of relativity is perhaps the most notable scientific breakthrough documented as having come about via a dream.

3. Passive Rest State (Idleness)
  i. Refreshing ease or inactivity after exertion or labour: *to allow an hour for rest.*
  ii. Relief or freedom, especially from anything that wearies, troubles, or disturbs.
  iii. A period or interval of inactivity, repose, solitude, or tranquility: *to go away for a rest.*
  iv. Mental or spiritual calm; tranquility.
  v. The repose of death: *eternal rest.*
  vi. Cessation or absence of motion: *to bring a machine to rest.*
  (From Dictionary.com)

I would like to draw your attention to the last item on the list: the cessation or absence of motion. The half-time break in a soccer or rugby match is a good example. The rest period ensures that the quality of play is maintained and hopefully the players will have enough energy left to make an exciting ending to the game.

Of course, our minds and emotions need rest too so having a break from your work and taking the time out for a tea or coffee is important for your well-being.

The Pomodoro Technique, a time management method developed by Francesco Cirillo in the late 1980s, uses a timer to break work up into intervals, usually 25 minutes in length, separated by short breaks of about five minutes. These intervals are regular breaks which aid assimilation and improve mental agility. The tricky part of this technique is that it works best when you are busy, which is when most people will be more likely to carry on working. This method therefore requires some testing of working in small bursts and seeing the improvements before it will become a habit. One important part of the technique is to use a timer and not rely on your memory. The recommendation if you test it for yourself is that in the five-minute break, simply grab a drink, sit back and chill or close your eyes and let them rest. The idler you are, the better. After you've completed four Pomodoro sessions, take a longer break of 30 minutes or so.

The video *Study Less, Study Smart*[3] is a highly informative presentation by Marty Lobdell that helps us understand the Pomodoro Technique. It eventually led to a book of the same title. Lobdell taught Psychology at Pierce College in Washington State for 40 years and has taught tens of thousands of students; he goes over and above his job description to assist students in reaching their potential and enjoying their studies. Lobdell says how in an academic environment students will spend hours studying yet often not in a way that works well for them.

---

[3] You can view the video at https://Findingthefulcrum.org or at https://youtu.be/IIU-zDU6aQ0

> *"The moment you start to slide, you're shovelling against the tide".*
> Marty Lobdell

He shares a study by the University of Michigan where students were requested to take note of the time they were about to start their study session and then note what time they felt their concentration ability drop off. The results revealed it was typically 25 to 30 minutes. Marty tells the story of Jeanette, a student whose grades dropped because of various circumstances. She made a conscious effort to make up the time by studying from 6pm to 12pm five nights of the week. One would expect that she would have aced everything but instead she went on to fail every single class. Jeanette had in reality experienced around 25 minutes of high-quality study followed by 5.5 hours of fatigue in which the gain from the first 25 minutes was lost.

Marty has a saying, 'the moment you start to slide, you're shovelling against the tide'. He also notes that the great thing is that small breaks of five minutes are all that's needed to refresh the mind. Had Jeanette known that, her six hours could have given her 5.5 hours of high-quality study. This is just one of many findings that Lobdell shares to help students work with the mind rather than against it.

I also learned that adding in some periods of 'aimlessness' between the times when I need my mind to be switched on is natural but not normal once we enter adulthood. We seem to disconnect from what childhood teaches about what reinvigorates us. We all know that small children get more emotional when they are forced to stay awake and naps are encouraged and even vital to their development. If 25 minutes is all an adult can realistically study for without needing a break, maybe we are not that dissimilar to children.

The idleness activities that help me reinvigorate include:
- Receiving an acupressure massage.
- Power napping.
- Chilling in a coffee shop reading up on the daily news.

Other people shared the following ideas:
- Window shopping.
- Walking in nature.
- Watching a favourite movie or TV series.

The idleness mantra is 'nothing to do, nowhere to go, no one to be'. Try it out a while and see what a huge difference it can make.

2. Active Rest State (Downtime)
   i. A time during a regular working period when an employee is not actively productive.
   ii. An interval during which a machine is not productive, such as during repair, malfunction, or maintenance. (From Dictionary.com)

You might imagine that in a business context downtime is viewed negatively as time equals money. However this is being questioned more and more as it's understood that employees are not as effective if they haven't rested enough.

More and more evidence is showing that downtime replenishes the brain's stores of attention and motivation; it encourages productivity and creativity, and is essential to both achieve our highest levels of performance and simply form stable memories in everyday life. A fatigued mind can be so unbalanced that we can't learn from the past or plan for the future. Moments of respite may even be necessary to keep one's moral compass in working order and maintain a sense of self.

I believe the best way to ensure this is to actively play. Give the mind a task that doesn't feel like a task, something that is enjoyable and pleasurable.

Marty Lobdell's findings on the efficiency of 25-minute study periods interspersed with five-minute breaks led him to wonder if the 30-minute cycle could be further improved. One innovation was to make the five-minute break focus on enjoyment, such as calling a friend for a brief catch-up or listening to a favourite song. I'm not sure why this works, maybe it's something like a reward system.

I remembered my breaks at primary school - the first thing I'd do is run out the door with a big smile. I loved to run for the sake of running. When I came back to class, I was alive, bright and fresh. I was invigorated.

From Lobdell's additional findings, I learned that play is much more important than we give it credit for. If we work hard and don't reward ourselves with the flood of good chemicals such as endorphins that come from fun and enjoyment, we could be interrupting our natural delayed gratification dynamics. Delayed does not mean no gratification; it is the balance of a reward in response to a given amount of effort.

The downtime activities that help me feel rewarded and reinvigorate me include:
- Watching a movie.
- Reading a book.
- Listening to comedy.

Other people shared these ideas:
- Playing with their pets.
- Completing puzzles.
- Craft work.
- Playing a game with their children.

As you can see, the emphasis is on being somewhat active but with fun and enjoyment as the primary goal.

1. Automicity

Let's start with a reminder:

Automicity = The act of intently taking ourselves off autopilot for a useful period of time.

We normally leave autopilot only when life catches us by surprise. The surprise is sometimes a welcome one and sometimes not. Generally speaking, it is the latter and is often termed a wake-up call; an unexpected bill, a health scare, being in a 'near miss' accident or the loss of someone close to us.

In Chapter 2.2, we experienced automicity through a combination of linguistic dynamics (the what works/what doesn't work questions) and defractionation. This made for a pause in the process of switching and cycling between asking ourselves 'what works for me' and 'what does not work for me'. It was a light hypnotic state that ironically helps us wake up from a trance that has kept us feeling stuck.

With the information gathered and outcomes of many experiences, I suspect that when we experience automicity as we did in Chapter 2.2, we experience something that links in with the processing ability of the fifth stage of sleep, REM. We activate our imagination to help us access areas of the subconscious that we want to learn from purposefully and we don't rely so much on the wild chance that our RAS radar picks this up.

I believe that when we **practice** automicity:

- We identify conflicts and things that no longer work for us. It's a bit like putting files in the trash on our PC. Each night, the operating system dumps the trash. In the same way, during REM our minds get to work on problems - and dump the trash.

- As eustress increases, we get even better at noticing (turning our RAS on) when we are effective (in our eustress zone) and when we need a break (in our distress zone).

- As we experience leverage (i.e. we tip our day more towards eustress), we stop creating so many of the problems and errors that come from operating when we're fatigued. We then have more time available to strike the balance with sleep and rest as we feel we need it.

In effect we are getting good at systematically clearing out our trash each day by purposefully practicing automicity to assist our REM each night. The compound effect of this leads to a greater sense of ease in one's life.

Summary

- Dreams in REM are for resolving problems, making sense of things, and learning. Automicity makes the most of REM by bringing issues into conscious awareness.

- Regular practice of automicity leads to sleep, rest and downtime habits that work for you and problems transform into solutions with increasing speed.

- Compounding the benefits of automicity and REM as part of a daily cycle allows us to drop what doesn't work for us and increase what does as we begin to see life more often through the filter of eustress.

In the next chapter we will look at the LAS™ Cycle and how we can bring more automicity into our day by making it into a habit in the form of a short daily practice. This synergy of factors will take very little time and bring us a great deal of value.

Recapitulation of Terms

Practice - repeated performance or systematic exercise for the purpose of acquiring practical skill or proficiency.

Purposeful Practice - Deliberate Practice + Systematic Practice.

Deliberate Practice - The skill of actively breaking down what we want to learn into specific parts, then researching and working on one element until we've made improvement before moving on to the next one. This builds depth.

Systematic Practice - Skilled repetition where we tap into daily, weekly, monthly cycles to build up a system that provides a process and structure that maximises the effects of repetition.

" Success is the sum of small efforts, repeated day in and day out. "

ROBERT COLLIER

Part 4

The Leverage Activation System (LAS™)

> "A bad system will beat a good person every time."
>
> W. EDWARDS DEMING

> The first rule of LAS: put natural learning first.
> The second rule of LAS: practice rule one.

KIERAN O'CONNOR

Aim To tap into the daily cycle so that we naturally and easily take full advantage of each day's learning.

Concepts
1. The Spiral Effect
2. LAS™ Cycle
3. Natural Timing

Chapter 4.1

The LAS™ Cycle

In Part 1 we applied ideo dynamics as leverage to break stress into two parts; bad stress which is distress and good stress which is eustress. This was the beginning of our journey where we increasingly tip the balance of our lives in favour of eustress. We also used our RAS to tap into our natural need for this healthy stress that stretches us in good ways.

In Part 2 we looked at the perceptual filter of 'what works'. This helped us distinguish the difference between autopilot and automicity, each having its own valuable uses.

We focused primarily on automicity which merges linguistic energetics and defractionation (a de-hypnosis technique). It allows us to untangle the things that work for us from the things that don't in a way that removes the underlying resistance that comes from forcing the mind. Automicity allows positive changes to unfold naturally.

We tested automicity to gain some experience in consciously taking ourselves off autopilot. We took this a step further by doing something that interrupts habitual nature, such as brushing our teeth with the non-dominant hand. Over time, these minutes of automicity will gradually compound and transform our autopilot so that it begins to work in our favour more of the time.

Automicity may feel different for you than it does for me. For me it was like when I am trying hard to think of something and the harder I try, the more the answer eludes me. When I give my mind a tea break instead, the answer pops up as if by magic.

Part 3 dealt with the perceptual filter of purposeful practice. This looked at how practice can shape us and give us some control over our future. We focused on deliberate and systematic practice so we could gain more skill. This is akin to learning how to learn.

As we gain skills with bringing these three parts more into our daily lives, our RAS will help us make the move from working hard to working smart. Distress will begin to diminish and eustress will increase.

Snakes and Ladders

Most of us have many ups and downs. The downs are a part of life and I have yet to meet someone who doesn't have some challenges. What you will discover is that by applying the Leverage Activation System™ (LAS) in a daily format, challenges will become more manageable as they won't last as long as they did before.

Figure 10 on the next page shows two spirals, one going upwards and the other going down.

We will still experience the downward spirals. Remember Snakes and Ladders? You probably played it when you were a child. It's an ancient game with origins in Nepal and Northern India. It has been played under many names including Gyan Chauper and Moksha Patamu roughly translating as 'the game of self-knowledge'. It has evolved over the generations and has retained the basic message: this is a game that teaches us how to manage and learn from the ups and downs of life. But what if life was less about avoiding problems and more about learning from them so quickly that they become every bit as valuable as our times on the upward spiral?

FIGURE 10

The Spiral Effect

THE ASCENDING SPIRAL	PRIMARY EMOTION[1]	SECONDARY EMOTION[1]
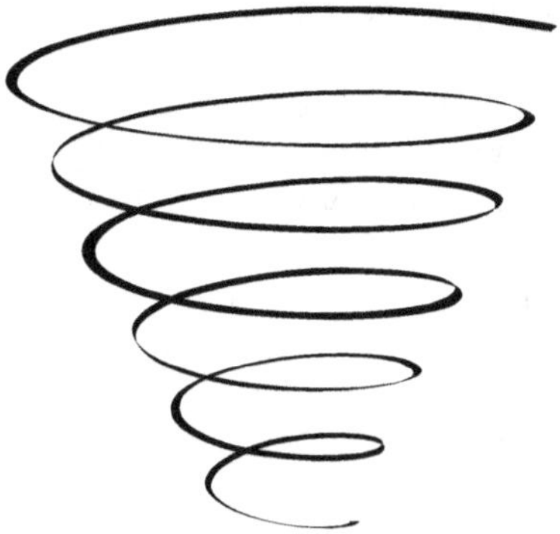	Love	Affection
		Lust
		Longing
	Joy	Cheerfulness
		Zest
		Contentment
		Pride
		Optimism
		Enthrallment
		Relief
	Surprise	Surprise

THE DECENDING SPIRAL	PRIMARY EMOTION[1]	SECONDARY EMOTION[1]
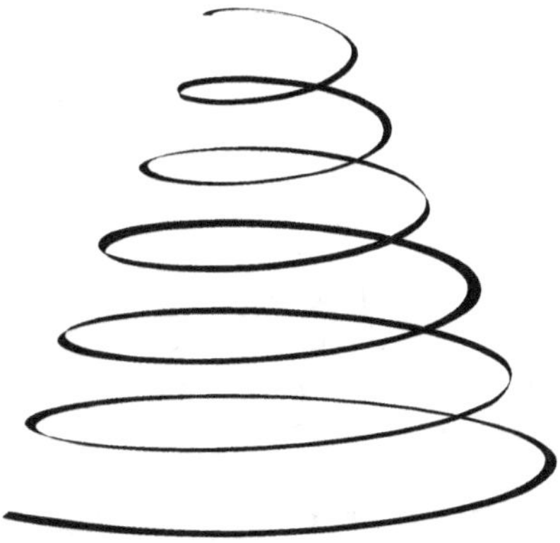	Anger	Irritation
		Exasperation
		Rage
		Disgust
		Envy
		Torment
	Sadness	Suffering
		Sadness
		Disappointment
		Shame
		Neglect
		Sympathy
	Fear	Horror
		Nervousness

[1] Primary and Secondary emotions as described in Shaver et al. (2001)

Engaging The LAS Cycle™

The Leverage Activation System™ (LAS) is the synergistic effect of the three perceptual filters that make up Parts 1, 2 and 3 of this book. This synergy helps us manage both the upward spirals and our day-to-day challenges.

In Figure 11, on page 196, we can see how Parts 1, 2 and 3 overlap. With the LAS cycle it really doesn't matter too much where you start out from. What matters most is that you start and then allow the cyclic and synergy effect to incrementally and naturally transform the downs to ups.

This is how I like to describe the synergy effect: apply one of the three and you get a bronze level of improvement. Apply two out of the three and you get silver. Apply all three and yep, you have guessed it… you get platinum.

"Hold on a moment," you say. "What about gold?" Well, you're correct, gold is what you get for bringing all three together; it's what you would gain just with having that synergy working for you. When you start infusing these three into your life daily, then you also benefit from the Dollar a Day compounding effect. So you go straight to platinum.

In Experience 6 back in Chapter 2.2 we had our first experience of automicity (which combined the 'what works' linguistic dynamic with defractionation mode) to loosen your habitual thinking. You were asked to fill in 10 rows in an alternating mode so you'd gain the experience, the learning and also stretch your eustress zone as a bonus. We will now complete a 'lite' version which taps into the power of compounding.

> **EXPERIENCE 8:** ENGAGE LAS LITE™
>
> Do this just as you did Experience 6 - switch between the 'what works for me' and 'what doesn't work for me' question but only focus on that day. So you'll fill in one example of something you did or experienced during the day that worked for you and then you write down something that didn't work for you. It's a 'lite' version of Experience 6.
>
> It is best if you do this exercise in the evening when you're starting to wind down as this is a sign that your melatonin levels are rising and it will signal to your subconscious that these examples are important to you and that you could do with its help!
>
> I've filled in a table already as an example.
>
> Please note that blank tables can be downloaded from http://www.findingthefulcrum.org.

Example: *Kieran O'Connor* _____ (name)

	WHAT WORKED FOR ME TODAY		WHAT DIDN'T WORK FOR ME TODAY
1	25-minute power nap after work and before exercise – it re-energised me.	2	Drank more than my usual single coffee in the morning – didn't enjoy the second one much.
3	Tested a blueberry, avocado and cacao smoothie – it was really tasty and super healthy.	4	Complained about traffic on the way to work – waste of my energy.
5	Called an old friend out of the blue for a 10-minute chat – laughed a lot.	6	Watched TV instead of working on an outline for an article on mastery – got stuck in an all or nothing mindset.

Example: _____ (name)

	WHAT WORKED FOR ME TODAY		WHAT DIDN'T WORK FOR ME TODAY
1		2	
3		4	
5		6	

This Lite version usually takes between 5 to 10 minutes, but if it takes longer don't be dissuaded. Actually, take it as encouragement because if you find it tricky to switch from one column to the next you are gaining a great benefit. It's also bringing underlying resistance to the surface.

FIGURE 11
The Leverage Activation System (LAS)

LAS is investment in incremental change by chipping away at what doesn't work for us because it does not align with our true nature. Lots of small subtle changes over time have a big effect.

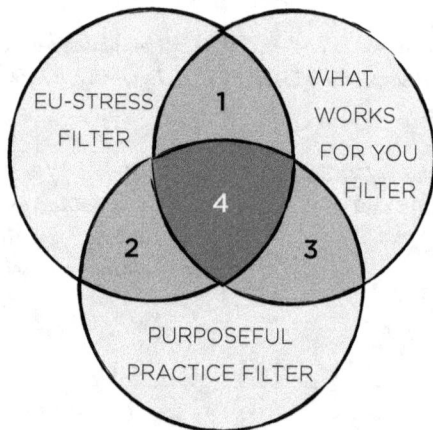

The LAS formula is based on three overlapping ingredients. Leave one out or be out of balance and you miss the full effect:

1. If you apply the Eu-Stress Filter and the What Works For You Filter, you will definitely get a one-off experience and a benefit. However without the Purposeful Practice Filter, you will not gain the benefit that is achieved from systematic practice.

2. If you apply the Eu-Stress Filter and the Purposeful Practice Filter, you will get some benefit just by checking in on how you feel on a regular basis. However without the What Works For You Filter, you will not gain the benefit that is achieved from de-fractionation.

3. If you apply the What Works For You Filter and the Purposeful Practice Filter, you will definitely get a gain by de-fractionation becoming a regular practice. However without the Eu-Stress Filter, you will not gain the full benefit that is achieved from your intuition guiding your way.

4. The centre symbolises where all three of the filters work together to provide a compunding effect. This synergy is what leads to naturally increasing your time with What Does Work For You and dropping and releasing What Does Not Work For You.

As you complete the sheet on page 195, you are completing two parts of the LAS™. Part 1 starts to transform distress into eustress; the more you tap into what works for you, the more good stress will become a part of your day. Part 2 is also included through the combination of automicity, the 'what works' question and defractionation. The third element is the repetition and practice element of LAS which we will come to soon.

Tapping into your Natural Timing

In Chapter 0 we looked at Natural Learning, now we will look at how we can tap into our natural sense of 'timing'.

A circadian rhythm is any biological process that displays an entrainable oscillation of about 24 hours. The term 'circadian' comes from the Latin circa, 'around', and dies, 'day', meaning literally 'about a day'.

You may have experienced a time when your own circadian rhythms have been interrupted, such as when the clocks change with the change of seasons or when you've travelled between different time zones.

Although circadian rhythms are biologically built in, they are entrained (adjusted and linked in) to the local environment by external cues. The most well-known cue is daylight which has the effect of turning on or turning off genes that control an organism's internal clock. NASA applies this for astronauts so they can still keep as many of the cycles as they would have on earth despite the body being in a weightless environment. Sleep patterns in space are very carefully calculated.

Circadian rhythms also influence hormone release, body temperature and other important bodily functions and so they are vital to our biological health. Abnormal and out of sync circadian rhythms have also been associated with areas such as obesity, diabetes, depression, bipolar disorder and seasonal affective disorder, more commonly known as SAD. Circadian rhythms also play a part in the reticular activating system (RAS) which is crucial for how we perceive the world (we looked at RAS in Part 0).

The primary circadian clock in mammals is located in the suprachiasmatic nucleus (SCN), a pair of distinct groups of cells located in the hypothalamus. Now don't be concerned, I am not expecting you to remember what SCN stands for! I have to use the idea of 'super charismatic nucleus' to help my own memory cope with this one.

The SCN receives information about illumination (traditionally daylight) through the eyes. The retina of the eye contains specialised cells which are photosensitive and project directly to the SCN where they help in the entrainment of this master circadian clock.

The SCN takes the information on the lengths of the day and night from the retina, interprets it, and passes it on to the pineal gland which in turn secretes the hormone melatonin. Secretion of melatonin peaks at night and ebbs during the day and its presence provides information about night-length.

> I believe that the RAS works even when we sleep and dream. Therefore, what we hold in mind later in the day is what tends to get carried over into sleep and, to some degree, the next day.

For most of us adults, melatonin levels start rising around 9pm. This is where we may feel that there is a transition between our waking state and the call of slumber. You might not go to bed at this time but it is usually where you naturally feel yourself winding down. One sign that the melatonin level is rising is when we feel that this day is crossing over into the next. It is as if we start to let go of the day's events and, if it was a typical day, we might even feel some haziness about what those events were. This is useful because it is the point where we can make the most of what is known as the Ebbinghaus Effect which we will cover later.

I believe that the RAS works even when we sleep and dream. Therefore, what we hold in mind later in the day is what tends to get carried over into sleep and, to some degree, the next day. Part of the reason I say this is that I have noticed my dreams tend to be biased towards what happens later in the day. The book I read before bed or a movie I watched will influence my dreams more than what happens earlier in the day.

I know that some school educational systems align homework with children's melatonin timing (which as expected is earlier than adults) so that they do their homework later in the evening (but not too late) to prepare them for the next day of school.

So, we can see that using the melatonin period is a way to tap into how we naturally learn. Of course, we want to learn how to time this best so we don't delay our sleep by leaving LAS Lite™ so late that we unsettle the end of our day.

Why do I need to do LAS Lite™ every day?

First, you don't have to do anything. Okay, you do need to breathe but even then your lungs are working automatically so you don't often need to be conscious of the act. So much so that you might not realise that the lungs work in reverse from the way most people think. The lungs actively push air out and passively breathe air in. I digress. Getting back to the question...

Science helps us work out the optimal time to complete LAS Lite™. Then we add in the compounding effect where we separate and combine to learn as much as we can from each day. Just as REM assists us at night, LAS Lite™ gives us a way to discern the things that worked for us so we can invite in more of the same. And as we continue to acknowledge the things that don't work for us, we'll gradually and incrementally stop feeding into them.

The subconscious mind is more impressed by small amounts of effort each day rather than one lump sum once a week. This is why I have made LAS Lite™ so easy to do - your subconscious resistance doesn't have much credence or leeway with this simple exercise.

So without further ado, let's go again and prove to your subconscious that you are willing to invest in a future that works for you and that you support and respect its need for gradual incremental change that aligns more and more with your true nature. All I ask of you is to do Experience 8 on one day and Experience 9 on the next - the night sleep in between is important.

EXPERIENCE 9: RE-ENGAGE LAS LITE™

This is the same as Experience 8. Apply it every evening as you wind down if you want to see the positive compounding effects of systematic practice in action.

Please note that blank tables can be downloaded from http://www.findingthefulcrum.org.

Example: *Kieran O'Connor* (name)

	WHAT WORKED FOR ME TODAY		WHAT DIDN'T WORK FOR ME TODAY
1	Helped a woman put heavy shopping into her car boot - enjoyed being of service.	2	Had a longer sleep but woke feeling groggy - slept a bit too long.
3	Completed an account's interim review - always makes for an easier end of year review.	4	Late for Kung Fu class - feel more prepared when I am on time.
5	Had a few beers with buddies while watching sport - had a great time.	6	Cut morning meditation short - was thinking too far ahead.

Example: _____ (name)

WHAT WORKED FOR ME TODAY	WHAT DIDN'T WORK FOR ME TODAY
1	2
3	4
5	6

Experience 9 moves on from Experience 8. It is the same process but now you have started to repeat the practice. You are engaging the perceptual filter of purposeful practice. You will have practiced many times in your life but probably haven't had many practice sessions that include automicity. Although this is only the second experience of LAS Lite™ it will already have started the compounding effect. **Every daily cycle counts.**

I invite you to complete this lite version every evening and time it as much as possible as your melatonin levels rise and you feel yourself winding down. You will be using defractionation to help you deconstruct and make sense of each day. And then your REM will complete the process.

My aim is to provide you with so much leverage that your subconscious feels the benefits as each day gets easier because of the magic of compounding. On a conscious level, you'll understand why it's worth the long-term investment. Eventually this will become a habit that works so well for you that not doing it would feel unwise. I personally miss only the rare occasional day but find that the 5-10 minutes each evening is highly valuable because it makes my days flow. This book is largely down to this daily practice as it allowed me time to write even while managing relationships, progressing a whole raft of projects, running a property portfolio and making the time and space for a demanding Kung Fu regime.

Difference between RAS and LAS

RAS is:

- Limbic-based.
- Helps us filter our view of the world based on what we believe will keep us alive.
- For most people, it is 100% automatic. They only come off automatic by chance or through a wake-up call from the external world.

LAS is RAS but it is also:

- Where we move off autopilot for a length of time.
- The leverage comes from how we bring together three elements that are useful on their own but more synergistically powerful when combined.
- Uses the RAS dynamic and directs it towards how we can drop more and more of what doesn't work and take on more and more good stuff.
- This is an incremental system that allows us to make steady, solid and permanent change while also drawing on the wisdom of what already works for us.
- This allows us to experience more and more eustress where we stretch ourselves doing the things that we enjoy most.
- This helps us follow the way of the water method.
- Fills our day with what works for us as much as is practically possible.

So, we can summarise this list by saying:

LAS is tapping into RAS by creating a new leverage perceptual filter.

Summary

- We are more linked into worldly cycles than we think.
- A daily cycle helps us learn the most from the day and improve the day to come. And so on.
- Apply LAS daily and see the benefits compound.

In the next chapter we will look at how we can gain leverage by focusing on the process rather than the outcome.

"Brothers, what we do in life echoes in eternity."

MAXIMUS DECIMUS MERIDIUS
(LEAD CHARACTER IN *GLADIATOR*)

Aim Developing a skilful practice mindset so that we integrate LAS™ more easily.

Concepts
1. The LAS Practice Model.
2. The Fifth Stage of Competence.
3. Dreyfus Model of Skill Acquisition.
4. Daily Discernment.
5. Invest In Loss.

Making Practice A Practice

By now you may feel like plugging your fingers in your ears whenever you hear the word 'practice'. But, because your subconscious is so impressed by effort and repetition, I will keep pushing so that your practice mindset is fully wired in.

Part 3 covered Purposeful Practice which focused on gaining foundational knowledge and expertise. Chapter 3.1 (You Become What You Practice) aimed to add a level of skill and quality to what you already practice so it becomes more natural to stop practicing things that don't work for you. What we leave out can prevent problems further down the road. We also looked at the deliberate elements of practice such as compounding and systematic practice and the various resting states.

This chapter applies LAS Lite™ as we want to fully engage the practice mindset. This is where we stop focusing on the outcome and focus on the process itself. When the journey moves to the forefront and the destination to the back, we will begin to work smarter rather than harder.

The Practice Mindset: The Fulcrum That Makes For Skill-Building

When we develop a new skill, we bring things together by creating a central link, a bridge between them or, in leverage terms, a fulcrum. In Figure 12, we can see that a desired ability has to be practiced as a skill before it becomes embedded as a habit, so skill bridges ability through to habit.

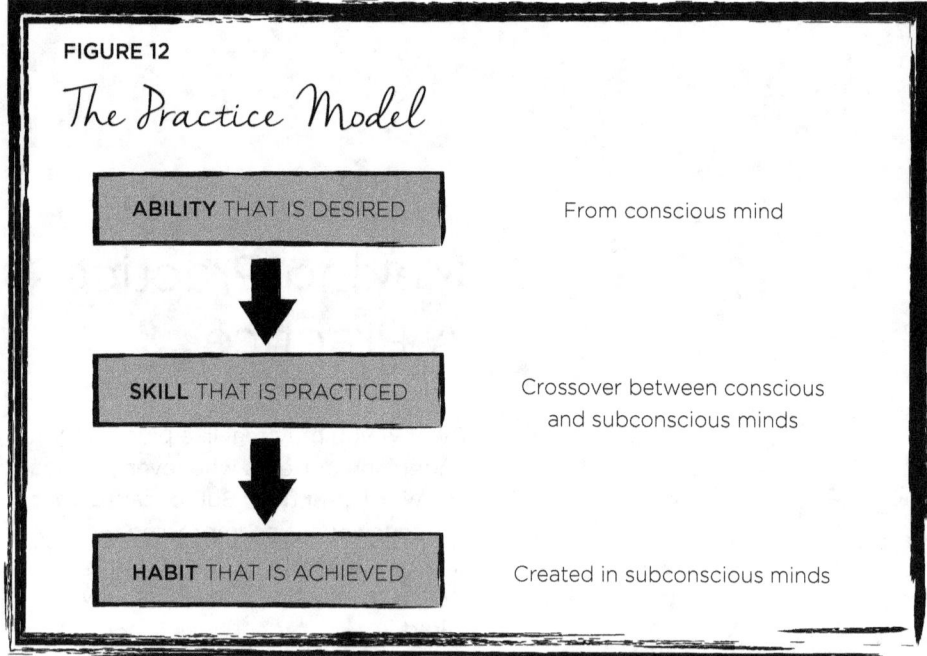

Building skills helps us achieve our goals but, as skill-building can be somewhat intangible, I'll share a personal example of a time when I experienced it in an unexpected way.

While I was living in Dublin I took the opportunity to stretch myself by learning salsa dancing. As a guy who was only ever comfortable dancing after a few beers to loosen up my inhibitions, this was quite a challenge but it turned out to be a very enjoyable learning experience.

The dance school broke the classes into four categories: Beginner, Improver, Intermediate and Advanced. This model worked well as it gave people a structure. Everyone knew where they slotted into the structure from the beginning and it also gave them a ladder of improvement to follow.

I moved quickly through the first two levels because my martial arts training helped me develop basic skills such as footwork, balance and timing. I followed the advice of my first martial arts teacher who'd said that classes were for learning and practice was what we applied in between classes. I left each class with a list of skills to work on and got to intermediate level much faster than expected.

All of us students could see that when we went up a level, we'd all be taken out of our comfort zones. We'd go from being very skilled in our current class to feeling very unskilled in the next level up. This gap became greater as the skill level increased. Due to a shortage of male students, an opportunity came up for me to move from intermediate to advanced way ahead of the time it would normally take. I accepted the move but was somewhat hesitant as salsa is a male-led art and the advanced class included female students who danced competitively.

Advanced level was just too much for me at that stage of my development and, after four weeks of persistence, I insisted on going back to intermediate classes. I was experiencing a 50/50 balance of eustress and distress and I simply wasn't enjoying the advanced level enough. There was too much new material balanced up against what I could do already. Also, the advanced classes required a higher time commitment than I could realistically offer with my demanding job.

The best thing I learned was how working in each of the four skill levels assisted me with my progress. Knowing what the difference was between the adjacent levels was so helpful for me in transcending them.

It was some years later that I discovered the Dreyfus Model which was originally used as a framework for the nursing and physician sectors. It was so useful that it was rolled out to a wide range of applications including the United States Air Force. It shows how perception, learning, study, practice, reasoning and rehearsal can all be built into one useful role-based model.

The Dreyfus model includes five roles that are based on skill level:
1. Novice.
2. Competent.
3. Proficient.
4. Expert.
5. Master.

Skill sets were broken down into the five roles providing a clear structure which:
a) Allows for a benchmark to be set for the roles.
b) Helps the student gauge how much time it will take them to progress through the roles.

    c) Provides a clear template that assists students if they get stuck at any stage.
    d) Allows for generalisation but also for the specific needs of individuals.

Item (a) is key as the ability to benchmark skills allows for very tangible crossover points for gauging a person's ability. Skills generally cannot be faked. It is clear to see why this model has been adapted by so many walks of life.

Applying the LAS™ Practice Model:
Ability, skill and habit are all related. Not sure what I'm getting at? I'll use my salsa example to explain further:

- **Desired ability:** To be able to lead the dance with a level of male certainty and security infused with feminine flow and finesse.

- **Skill that is practiced:** The rudiments of footwork, timing and basic movements that more and more lead from focus on movements to focus on movement itself.

- **Habit that is achieved:** 80% focus on what is well drilled and practiced and 20% on fun and flow to play with new ideas and spontaneity.

At this point, it might be in idea to take a few moments just to consider the ability, skill and habit relationship that might have drawn you to reading this far. If no answers pop up, you might discover that daily discernment will naturally help bring them to the surface as you progress.

> Insanity: doing the same thing over and over again and expecting different results.
>
> ALBERT EINSTEIN

Daily Discernment: The Most Fundamental Skill Of All

When people read or hear this Einstein quote, they often think it applies to someone else as we all believe that we are totally sane. How else would we manage to get through life if we weren't?

Do you remember your 'what works for you' and 'what doesn't work for you' lists back in Part 2? You did this as a list initially just so you'd feel how the mind normally works through making links and associations. Then you switched between both questions which allowed you to experience how the mind feels when it is taken off autopilot.

I'm sure that you will have come up with at least one thing in your life that does not work for you. Therefore, my friend, you can join me in being somewhat insane. If you know that something doesn't work for you, why would you keep on doing it? In fact I will make a deal with you. If one of the things on the 'doesn't work for me' list is less than one day old, then you have a pass to get out of your padded cell free. That's fair, isn't it?

When you started LAS Lite™ in the last chapter, we shifted from looking at what generally does and doesn't work for you to what you experience during that day. Clearing up the 'what doesn't work' list every day gives you a fair crack at the whip of attaining a more sane and serene mind.

> The downside of this right and wrong, good and bad mindset is that you have been trained to see things as polarities...

There's a good reason for doing LAS Lite™ every day (and I think Mr Einstein would give it the sanity vote): LAS Lite™ works for you because you are human. Your mind is based on duality because when you were very small, authority figures - all with the best intentions - taught you right from wrong. This would have initially been with things like naked flames and hot surfaces and would have progressed to things like not talking to strangers or playing near traffic. It was vital to learn this as it kept you safe.

The downside of this right and wrong, good and bad mindset is that you have been trained to see things as polarities such as up/down, hot/cold, under/over, and left/right. Again, this is all well and good but there is another downside. Conflicts happen when one thing does not agree with another, some are obvious like when one country does not agree with another and goes to war. But other human conflicts are not so obvious.

One example that made an impression on me comes from a movie called *Fight Club*. One of the scenes involved the two main characters: Tyler Durden played by Brad Pitt and the Narrator and main character played by Edward Norton. Durden is a renegade and leads the disillusioned Norton character through a series of experiences to attempt to turn off his autopilot thinking. Late one night, they come across a young Asian man who is studying through the dark hours while working at an all-night store. Durden pulls a gun and the shop assistant is told to put down his maths book and move to the rear of the premises. The man is forced to lie flat on the ground with a revolver to his head. Durden calmly says that he is going to kill him but, just out of curiosity, he wonders what the man had always dreamed of being. Without hesitation and with nothing to lose, the shop assistant reveals he'd always wanted to be a veterinarian. Pitt removes the gun and tells him that if he doesn't fulfil his dream, he will track him down and finish the job.

Although this is an extreme example, we can see that the Asian man had a conflict about what he wanted to do with his life and needed a wake-up call to get him off his autopilot path. The gap between his conscious and subconscious mind was so large and the denial so strong that he had forgotten his dream. One reason that people stick to a path that is not aligned with their true nature is the fear that what they have done up to this day will be lost. With LAS, this fear can be acknowledged and, rather than fighting or denying it, it can be transformed step by step.

How can this happen? Discernment is the ability to judge well, the ability to tell the difference between truth and error. Without this functioning for you, you'll find that Einstein's version of insanity is your daily companion and reminder. Of course, this is not helped by the good/bad mindset as no one is ever going to score 100% for discernment. We all live in the grey area that exists in the spectrum between black and white. The great news is that with LAS, we can incrementally learn daily discernment and make the most of our life experience from dusk till dawn. The old saying 'don't throw the baby out with the bathwater' is all about the skill of discernment.

Now seems a good time to reveal to you how the combination of the 'what works for you'/'what doesn't work for you' defractionation process has a very clever effect which is so subtle that it might fall into the elusive obvious category.

The Affirmative Mind

It is well understood in hypnosis that the mind is affirmative in nature. For example, if I ask you not to think of a pink elephant, you have to think of a pink elephant as a reference and a contrast in order to try not to think of it. So to 'not think' is impossible for us.

When you ask 'what doesn't work for me', your mind also has to refer to the things that work for you. This happens instantaneously, so we miss it. But our RAS sees it and learns from it at a subtle level. With the automicity dynamic, you are bringing this cognition up into your conscious mind during which a learning opportunity takes place as the neural connection is exercised and re-enforced. If we go through the LAS Lite™ process often enough, new dendrites will grow and the old ones lose their focus. There is no unlearning; there is only an untangling and then a new learning. With daily repetition of LAS Lite™ a space opens up which maximises learning that happens on a subtle yet powerful level.

The compounding effect loosens up the habits that support 'what doesn't work' in our lives. So if you're concerned about reminding yourself of what doesn't work, stop! If you only asked yourself the 'what doesn't work' question, the lack of defractionation could drive you down a negative path. This one-sided way of questioning the mind is what makes for a problem mindset while defractionation leads to a solution mindset. It's good to be open and honest. In biblical terms we are taught: The truth shall set you free.

With LAS™ and daily LAS Lite™, not only do we get more of 'what works' from what already works for us because of the automatic affirmation function of the mind, we also learn from what doesn't and set our RAS to take the learnings and make them work for us.

Now if that doesn't convince you to spend a maximum of 10 minutes a day with LAS Lite™ you might be in need of a neatly fitting white jacket with lots of straps to keep your arms out of mischief!

The Fifth Stage Of Competence

In Chapter 0, we looked at replacing habits and the four stages of competence. The fifth stage is rarely discussed perhaps because it is the true mastery level. It is described by many as 'conscious competence of unconscious competence'. This is a trait of leading edge thinkers who see right to the heart of complex principles and concepts and combine them to create simple patterns, structures and processes.

The fifth stage makes me think of those people who teach well and those who can't teach even though they have mastered the skills. One of my friends, a part-time ski instructor, is one of those great teachers. I was amazed at how good he was at breaking all the skills down into smaller skills before building them up again to suit each individual learner. It seemed intuitive. I told him how much I enjoyed his teaching and he jokingly replied that it was only because he had zero natural skiing ability himself and so hadn't been able to skip any stages when he was learning. He knew first-hand the challenges that students faced and he was able to figure out how to work through each of these in a way that would work for everyone.

When we practice LAS Lite™ daily, we begin to find simplicity where others see complexity. The practice even allows us to make simplicity itself a skill. Those without this process may be really good learners - in reality we are all good learners - it is just that with LAS Lite™, we tap into our inner nature and only compare ourselves with our past selves. We use others to gauge our progress but we do not compare. When we compare, the duality of the mind tells us we are either better or worse than them and this robs us of the vital energy we get from true discernment.

Setting Up Your RAS Fulcrum (What You Do) And Pivot (When You Do It)

Conscious skill-building and the practice mindset allows a person to see the fulcrum and pivotal points that other people miss.

One example of this comes from a TV series that starred Gordon Ramsay, the world-renowned chef. Each episode he visited a struggling US restaurant and tried to get it back on track. It was as if he followed the same recipe for each place and it was very effective because he encountered the same problem everywhere: the restaurant owner had lost their way and could not see how. There would always be a moment where the restaurant owner had to face some kind of denial and it was Gordon's job to use his bag of tricks to bring this about.

The episode that stood out for me was about a restaurant that had once been very successful but was now losing so much trade that bankruptcy was a distinct possibility. The male owner had even made the conscious decision to buy frozen produce to save on overheads.

Gordon secretly requested the two browbeaten chefs to go local and buy fresh sea produce. The restaurant had a prestigious and panoramic ocean front position so this made sense. With such a breathtaking ocean view, anything on the menu less than 'caught that day' would be missing a huge opportunity. Then he asked them to make up some meals from the ingredients but to keep this a secret so that the owner believed Gordon had done all the work. The owner and his wife were amazed at how good the food was and aggressively turned on the two chefs asking why they couldn't do the same. In their eyes, the chefs were obviously the ones at fault. This was exactly what Gordon had planned for. He revealed that the chefs had chosen the menu, picked the produce and done the cooking. Plus they'd proved that fresh produce was more cost-effective than frozen because it was right on their doorstep. He pointed out that if they served fresh daily produce, the costs of the restaurant would take care of themselves.

Once the two chefs were given their opportunity, they turned the restaurant around in no time at all. In my opinion, the freshness of produce was the **fulcrum point** in this example. The **pivotal point** was the moment when the owners were carefully orchestrated into looking for someone to blame, and then realised that the true blame (responsibility in reality) was clearly to be placed on their own shoulders. They were conned in a helpful way into facing their own denial in such a way that the truth was beyond question.

As you apply the Leverage Activation System™ (LAS) daily via LAS Lite™, you will become more skilled at picking up on fulcrum and pivotal points. The fulcrum points are where you can intervene and make a change and the pivot points tell you when to make those interventions.

As these coincide more and more outside of yourself, you will be able to recognise them inside yourself in terms of habitual thinking. An ability to apply timely adjustments will prove very valuable.

Invest In Loss

Daoist students do not worry about making mistakes like most people do; honing their skills is a much higher priority to them than how they appear to others. They don't purposely fail at things or get sloppy in their practice because of this lack of concern. They strike a balance between doing their best while also understanding that long-term learning is more important than a single success or failure. Thus the term 'invest in loss'.

When you have a daily practice such as LAS Lite™, you become so good at learning from life that you naturally feel more comfortable with taking risks. This is because the risks are more and more in alignment with what already works for you so, ironically, they are not really risks... they are more like opportunities.

Summary

- Skills and skill-building are the bridges between the things we want in life and the habits that will bring those things to us.

- Daily discernment is the fundamental skill for a sane mind.

- Seeing the fulcrum and pivotal points in life can help us develop the habit of working smart rather than working hard.

In the next chapter we will look at how to make the most of what the mind is really good at and re-assign what it's not so good at.

> Memory... is the diary that we all carry about with us.

OSCAR WILDE

Aim Make the most of how we remember (and forget) to maximise the effectiveness of LAS™.

Concepts
1 The Ebbinghaus Effect.

2 The Richness of Ritual.

Reminding Your Mind

Memory is not all that it seems. Human memory is a science in itself and, with an aging population, forgetting and forgetfulness dynamics are receiving a lot of attention.

Hermann Ebbinghaus was an early twentieth century German psychologist. In 1885, Ebbinghaus came up with a hypothesis on the exponential nature of forgetting. His aim was to demonstrate what happens when we learn something but do not use repetition to help us retain the information. As obvious as this sounds, saying one person has a good memory and someone else's memory is poor is not comparing like with like if only one of them has used repetition to help them remember. Both memories may be equally strong (or poor); it's the repetition that's truly important.

Ebbinghaus focused his studies on transience which is the natural process of forgetting that occurs with time. The subconscious mind forgets what we do not make an effort to remember. If we don't make some effort to highlight the importance of what we've learned the subconscious deems it unimportant and it is soon overtaken by what is perceives to be more important matters.

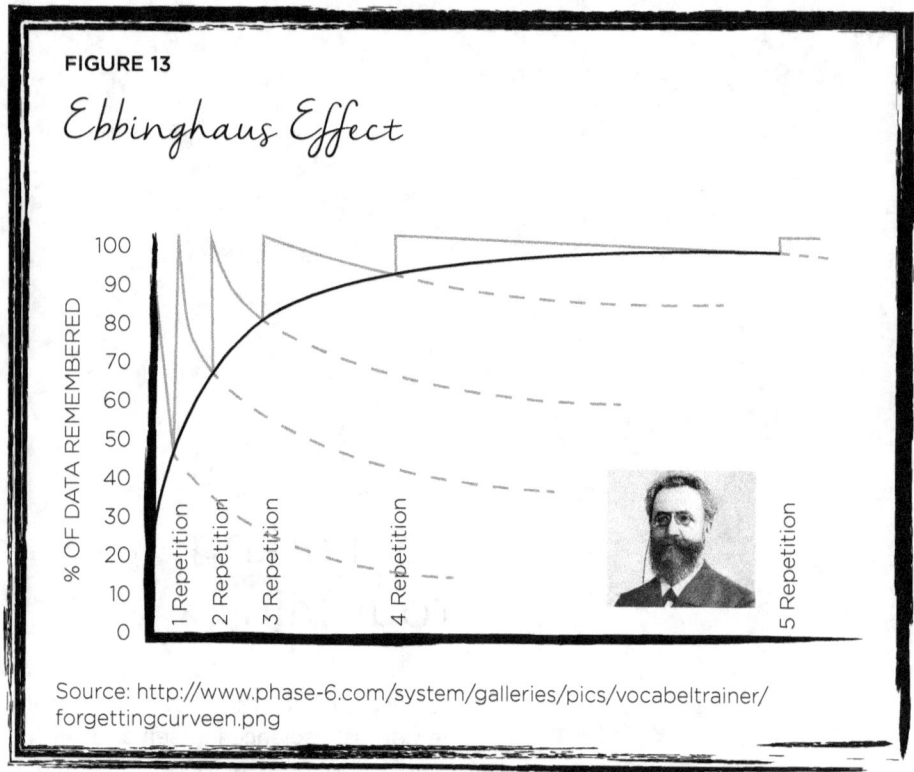

Source: http://www.phase-6.com/system/galleries/pics/vocabeltrainer/forgettingcurveen.png

It's probably no surprise to you that when we review, relearn and recap, we assist our learning process. This means that if we learn something new and do not follow it up at all, the new information will be lost within days, weeks and months. Here are some more of the key points from Ebbinghaus's work:

a. **How we best remember.**
Workplace training courses rarely make use of the scientific findings about memory. It's seldom that training courses are followed up by a set of shorter sessions at defined intervals. If they did, those courses would look like this as an example:

i. Initial training: five days.
ii. First follow-up: a month later for half a day.
iii. Second follow-up: three months later for two hours.
iv. Third and final follow-up: six months later for one hour.

These extra sessions would be less about aiming for a 100% retention rate and more about using the intervals to both remind us and focus on the most helpful content from the initial training when it is rolled out into the real world. The follow-ups could be via media such as teleconferencing or even in packages which the attendees complete in their own space and time.

You can do this for yourself with this book. When you've finished it, set a date to reread it (or parts) in a few weeks or months - the curve in Figure 13 shows how much this will boost your retention rate.

If you want to test Ebbinghaus's retention findings, why not add some reminders in your diary to come back and either reread this book or some selected chapters. It's best if you write the dates down in advance rather than relying on your memory!

b. The best time to refresh your learning is when you are just about to forget.
Here's an example of the elusive obvious if ever there was one! At first this totally confused me and reading this sentence felt like reading a puzzle. Then I wondered if the memory muscles are like physical muscles where resting is critical between workouts if we want to get the best out of them. But also, too long a break between workouts is inefficient. Then, the optimal timing for refreshing the memory made complete sense.

You already make use of this mechanism in your daily LAS Lite™ practice. When your melatonin kicks in every evening, you will already be starting to forget a lot of your day. This is why it's the best time to complete your LAS Lite™ practice.

How We Best Remember To Forget

Ebbinghaus's findings are less about the skill of remembering and more about the skill of forgetting. It may well be that when we are going about our daily business on autopilot, we are subconsciously **trying to forget** what does not work for us rather than **learning from it**. This of course cannot work as we are still giving it attention and keeping it alive. I believe that when a true learning is made, a resolution of the mind takes place. This allows us to be done with what doesn't work and file it in the trash where it belongs.

Forgetting is very important for letting go of what no longer works for us so perhaps we should become very skilled at it. The first thing to bear in mind is that forgetting can be passive or active.

a. Passive forgetting happens when we are never reminded of something and the dendrites in the brain die over time, usually over months and years.

b. Passive forgetting often occurs when we deny and suppress our hurts and disappointments because we don't have an effective way to process and resolve them.

c. Active forgetting can be applied with a tool such as LAS Lite™ to effectively resolve issues daily instead of hoping that passive forgetting or our REM will take care of them for us.

d. Active forgetting is a skill that we can build.

The Richness of Ritual

Before we discuss ritual in detail, let's look at the meaning of the word.

1. An established or prescribed procedure for a religious or other rite.
2. A system or collection of religious or other rites.
3. Observance of set forms in public worship.
4. A book of rites or ceremonies.
5. A book containing the offices to be used by priests in administering the sacraments and for visitation of the sick, burial of the dead, etc.
6. A prescribed or established rite, ceremony, proceeding, or service: *the ritual of the dead.*
7. Prescribed, established, or ceremonial acts or features collectively, as in religious services. (Taken from Dictionary.com)

A ritual can also be any activity that we perform for its practical value or because the act in itself represents and emphasises some meaning that we consider important.

Rituals are all around us: playing the national anthem before a sporting event, wearing caps and gowns at graduations, preparing a candlelit dinner; these are all rituals and are designed to focus our attention. In religious circles, the use of daily, weekly and seasonal rituals are used to structure the year. There are also additional pivotal ceremonies to mark the major life transitions of birth, adulthood, marriage and death.

Ritual symbols are powerful because they speak the same language as the subconscious mind, which speaks in pictures. So when we ritualise something, it is like ditching the flashlight and turning on a laser.

I believe that ritual acts have five main uses:

- They can structure our days, weeks, and years.
- Rituals help us give our subconscious mind a way of distinguishing daily chores from what we consider to be most important to us.
- They give shape to public expressions of powerful emotions: grief at funerals and joy at weddings, graduations, birthdays and anniversaries.
- They help to reorient and stabilise our own feelings when we need to comprehend and cope with crucial life passages.
- They help separate the important from the unimportant. Or, to put it another way, what works for us and what does not.

What distinguishes an activity from a ritual? I think we use ritual when we have some investment in how an activity or event will affect our future. The ritual is a way of symbolising its increased importance.

In Chapter 2.1, we touched briefly on Elisabeth Kübler Ross's work on the five stages of grief. Loss and grief are usually associated with bereavement and most of us receive some catharsis from attending our loved one's funeral, our society's ritual to mark a person's passing. But losses come in many forms and unfortunately we often don't have a conventional ritual to support us through these events. Redundancy, having something stolen, or even a disappointing grade at school are all losses and all have their effects. Finishing my engineering degree course was a loss experience for me as it had required so much of my focused attention. It took quite some time to get back to a 'normal' life.

Handling loss is itself a rite of passage. How we are taught to handle losses as children, such as the death of our family pets, can set up how we handle losses in later life.

LAS as a daily practice is a form of ritual which helps us work through the small losses we experience when we have to let go of a part of ourselves, such as the items on our 'what doesn't work' list. I didn't mention this earlier because I wanted you to experience the ritual yourself on more of a subconscious level before gaining this conscious understanding.

Rituals can work for you

Do you recall Marty Lobdell in Chapter 3.3 and how he helped students improve their study habits? You'll remember how research showed that a 25-minute study period followed by a five-minute rest period allowed the students to maximise their study time. The five-minute breaks that focused on fun improved their studies even more.

Lobdell shared findings from research by the University of Hawaii that really caught my attention. Researchers asked students to tell them about their biggest problem with studying. The number one response was 'we can't get into it'. Most of the students lived in dorm rooms which made it tricky to focus on their studies as it is a multifunctional and multi-occupant room. Not a great place to study! The professor at the University of Hawaii upon hearing this had a realisation and an idea. He noticed that all the dorms had a table lamp and he offered a suggestion: adding a little sign to it that said 'study lamp'. They would use the lamp for study only and use the other lights for everything else. They would switch the light on when their study period started and switch it off when they took a break and at the end of the study session. The students that followed this guidance generally moved up by one grade point by the end of the next term.

There are many theories about why a sign on a lamp could give this measurable and impressive improvement. I think it's because it taps into the ritualistic element of the mind and the lamp came to symbolise how important and valuable study time was for the students' future.

How could you use ritual to open and close your daily LAS Lite™ practice so that you can signal its importance to your subconscious mind? This is how I do it:

> **a. Opening:** As per Chapter 2.3, towards the end of the day when the melatonin is kicking in, I brush my teeth equally with both my dominant and non-dominant hand.
>
> **b. LAS Lite™:** I complete the LAS Lite™ on a notepad with a high-quality blue pen which is a pleasure to write with.
>
> **c. Closing:** I say the Serenity Prayer (based on Reinhold Niebuhr's quote in chapter 2.2) which is special to me because it embodies discernment. If you don't know it already or recall it, it goes:
>
> **God, grant me the serenity to accept the things I cannot change; courage to change the things I can; and the wisdom to know the difference.**

I break LAS Lite™ into three parts because the mind has a way of looping so that when we make a mental sandwich, it's the middle part that is forgotten faster by the conscious mind but made more important to the subconscious mind. All ceremonies will follow this pattern to some degree.

Summary

- Actively forgetting what no longer works for us is elusive yet it is a skill that can be developed.

- Rituals help us give our subconscious mind a way of distinguishing daily tasks from what we consider to be most important to us.

- LAS Lite™ works even better if you turn it into a simple ritual such as brushing your teeth before you do it and saying a prayer afterwards.

In the next chapter we will review our journey by applying a very clever trick that has made motor vehicle reliability (amongst many other things) improve dramatically over the past 20 years.

Recapitulation of Terms

Leverage Activation System™ (LAS) - a synergy of three elements which are the perceptual filters that form Parts 1, 2 and 3 of this book. It makes for a very effective and natural way to transform the day-to-day challenges in life into valuable opportunities that we can learn from.

LAS Lite™ - a daily activity that takes between 5-10 minutes. The compounding effect of LAS Lite™ means that, in leverage terms, it gives way more value than you would ever think given the time expended.

Daily Discernment - The fundamental skill that restores sanity by incrementally allowing us to see more clearly what doesn't work for us and what does.

> Success is not final, failure is not fatal: it is the courage to continue that counts.

WINSTON CHURCHILL

Part 5

The Final Hypnotic Installment

> "The only source of knowledge is experience."
>
> ALBERT EINSTEIN

> Basically, if I have no intention of using a service then I won't bother reverse engineering it.

JON LECH JOHANSEN

Aim To help our subconscious learn by walking back over the path we have taken together.

Concepts Reverse engineering.

Chapter 5.1

Reverse Engineering Our Way Back

Asia's sudden rise to prominence in car and electronics manufacture is one good example of reverse engineering. Towards the end of the twentieth century, Asian companies took, stripped down, and copied Western goods in a very smart application of the Daoist separate and combine principle. This initially led to lots of poor fakes but it didn't stop there. As cars and other goods were stripped down and rebuilt, Asian firms began to find the areas of unreliability that were hidden within the technology. This reverse engineering of Western technology led to a huge shift in the automotive and electronic markets and Eastern manufacturers became pre-eminent, their products increasingly known for their reliability. Eventually the West had to sit up and ask exactly what they were missing.

In my first year of apprenticeship I had to do foundation training in general engineering. One of the projects was to strip a car engine and rebuild it. This confused me because I was initially training to be an electrical technician and not a mechanic, but my instructor said: 'If you want to really understand engineering it might be wise to understand how an engine works.' He said that the best way to learn was to strip down the engine and rebuild it lots of times, but once would be enough for me to get the gist. I was extremely proud (and amazed) when my rebuilt engine started first time.

This chapter takes a similar approach - we will look back though the book in reverse order to gain a leveraged perspective on what we've learned about leverage itself. By the end of the chapter I hope that you will have a gained a valuable appreciation and understanding of this Eastern idea. Experiencing just how helpful a reverse perspective can be might well activate your RAS so you will start to notice where this could usefully be applied in your day-to-day life.

Part 4

In this section, the Leverage Activation System™ (LAS) brought together Parts 1, 2 and 3. LAS taps into the Reticular Activation System (RAS) which is the part of the mind that generalises, distorts, and deletes what we pick up from the world via our senses.

LAS Lite™ is best done at the end of the day when melatonin levels increase and we're beginning to experience the onset of sleepiness. REM, the fifth stage of the sleep cycle, **separates out** what we have learned throughout our dream period. LAS Lite™ and REM work together beautifully to maximise our natural problem-solving abilities.

Day after day, applying LAS Lite™ loosens the habits that don't work for us; bit by bit we chip away at them. At the same time, we affirm what works for us and, over time, our days are gradually filled with more good stuff that leads to more eustress. Gently turning our attention to the things we do every day, and acknowledging the positive habits as well as the negative, can change our lives for the better as we tap into the wisdom that each of them can provide for us.

Part 3

We looked at the perceptual filter of purposeful practice, the way that practice has shaped us up to now and how we can tap into it to take a measure of control over our future. In reality **practice is what we do every day** because our subconscious mind is a re-enforcement system. A practice mindset is one that focuses on the journey rather than the outcome.

We investigated deliberate and systematic practice so that we could use both elements more skilfully and naturally.

With purposeful practice, first we become aware of the parts of our lives that need practice and then we do what we need to do. It also allows us to tap into our natural need for healthy stress that stretches us in good ways.

Part 2

Here we looked at the perceptual filter of 'what works for you' and two dynamics of the mind - autopilot and automicity. We'd be lost without autopilot: we use it most of the time and it plays a vital role in our lives. It can however get us into all kinds of trouble if allowed to run away with itself.

Automicity, a way of helping the mind use discernment, was practiced so that making **informed choices** becomes more of an application of skill rather than an occasional accident. It allows us to get better at dropping what doesn't work for us while keeping and enhancing the things that do.

We also experienced the fact that automicity slows us down. It's a skilful way to interrupt the mind and delve down into the subconscious both kindly and respectfully.

'What works' is a helpful question that, combined with defractionation (a de-hypnosis technique), allows us to separate the things that do not work for us from the things that do. We also began a daily practice to see how we can use existing habits as foundations for building new ones. This is the vital skill of Daily Discernment.

Part 1

An ideo dynamic was applied as a form of leverage to break stress into two parts, bad stress which is also known as distress and good stress which is also known as eustress. Eustress = healthy stress that **stretches** our abilities in good ways. We need it if we want to live a healthier, happier and more fulfilling life.

This laid the ground for the remainder of the book as the main aim was to find ways to tip the balance of our lives towards eustress.

Part 0

Here we looked at seven basic facts on how the mind works. These are seven of many and were selected so they would help build a foundation for the rest of the book. We initially looked at **Natural Learning** as this book aims to tap into your true nature by using what nature gives us, including leverage, e.g. you use the lever of your arm whenever you brush your teeth.

Delayed gratification was crucial to this section which then went on to explore perceptual filters. As a person who invests your time in reading, you probably already knew that we place value and importance on what we have to work for. We understand the nature of investment because at some point we have all experienced long-term efforts coming to fruition. You've invested time in this book because you wanted to use leverage to shift the balance of your life so you experience more good stuff more of the time.

Reliability was highlighted as a key factor in delayed gratification. In our early years when we were most easily influenced, it's likely that we received mixed, conflicting, and confusing messages which would have interfered with this vital dynamic of trust. Now we know about that, we can take a measure of control over it. We can learn to trust our ability to discern.

Part -1

Separate and Combine was the first of the Daoist ideas that we looked at. This is the basis of all effective learning.

The water method, the second of the Daoist ideas, was contrasted with the fire method which uses force to create change and usually ends up making more problems that we have to use our valuable energy to resolve. The water method is not passive; rather it gently encourages us to work with our own ebbs and flows so we can find the path of **least resistance**.

The last of the Daoist ideas was 'the problem isn't where you think it is'. It points out that we are all biased because everything we see is affected by what we already have in our minds. We can learn to get out of our own way by understanding that we innocently operate from habits, and some of these work for us while others don't. If we can be open to the idea that what worked for us yesterday does not necessarily work for us today, we develop a state of super-fluidity. This fluidity lets us move from a problem mindset to a solution mindset where we still have problems in life, but they become less permanent and more adaptable and informative in nature.

We then looked at the Elusive Obvious and hypnosis. Hypnosis is a study of how the conscious and subconscious minds relate to each other. When the conscious and subconscious relate effectively, they are coherent. No problems can be experienced... only solutions. Increasing **coherence** allows us to get out of our own way and tap into the natural flow of life.

Leverage came next. We explored various forms of leverage however it is the decision-making ability that comes from the relationship between the conscious and subconscious that is the most important. Making truly informed decisions via coherence is a skill that cannot be ignored.

This book aims to re-establish communication that is based on aligning our own true nature with nature itself.

In the next chapter we will look at ideas that add the natural powers of compounding to your efforts.

> Reward yourself each month for a weekly task so that you will do better daily.

KIERAN O'CONNOR

Aim To apply compounding by tapping into informed enthusiasm.

Concepts
1 Losada Ratio.

2 The Power of Picture Proof (a picture is worth a thousand words).

Chapter 5.2

Compounding Your Gains

Chapter 3.2 looked at compound interest and talked about how we want to allow time to work in our favour and assist our growth as much as possible. This led us to a daily practice. LAS Lite™ takes a very short time but because of a number of factors plus the fact that we do it every day, it has a compounding effect each time it's done.

It takes time to wire in habits so let's look at how we can make the most of our natural motivation.

Recognition And Reward Cycle

Up to now we've worked on a daily circadian cycle basis. Now we'll cast our nets wider and look at weekly and monthly cycles and how these three can be linked together to compound the benefits each can bring to each other.

As you can imagine, when we look to make changes over longer periods of time where the improvement, goal or achievement is further away from where we initially start, we find that we naturally need a greater incentive. Remember the marshmallow experiments?

When we are establishing a new habit, we need all the help, support or even tricks that can assist the 'bedding-in-period' for the new habit. This is especially so where the nature of the habit is so well linked in with our autopilot mechanism that weeks or months are required to achieve the state where the new habit feels more natural than the previous habit. Any resistance experienced during this transition is itself very natural. This resistance is linked with the four phases of competence.

What can help enormously is to apply a delayed gratification mindset to help us move through the transitional period when we need motivation to keep us on track into the time when the habit has been fully installed. It is the trust in achieving greater satisfaction that allows us to hang in there if and when the going gets tough.

There are a number of ideas about how long it takes a person to establish a new habit. Although the statistics vary, we know that both recognition and reward are part of the human motivation system although they operate mostly below our conscious level of awareness.

I want to share a simple yet elegant weekly recognition and monthly reward idea with you. The beauty of it is that even when you become consciously aware of how it works, the way that it fits in with your daily cycle is so natural you will wonder how this has eluded you. I certainly wondered about that

Weekly Recognition

Born in 1939, Marcial Losada, a Chilean psychologist, consultant and research director, worked on the 'positivity balance'. He conducted many experiments on the ratio of positivity to negativity that people experienced and said there was an observable cut-off point - 2.9013. Anything below this figure represented a downward spiral of failure and anything above indicated an upward spiral of success. For ease of purpose, the figure was rounded off to three.

I'll share some information on the Losada Ratio with you but please be aware that his ideas have received mixed feedback. I suggest you do your own research and make up your own mind. Personally, I've found the Losada Ratio very helpful although I don't focus so much on the ratio itself which I believe to be very contextual.

The general idea is that when we are in an environment where we receive positive feedback at a ratio of 3:1 or above, we feel energised and motivated. Below 3:1 and we become disenchanted and our productivity falls. Losada noted that organisations where the 3:1 minimum had not been achieved tended to be in decline.

The 3:1 ratio is called 'the flourishing range' by some. Leading thinkers and companies such as Google maintain an environment of something like 6:1. This is made up of a culture where:

- People are trusted to do a great job and do not clock in and out each day.
- During lunch times, guest speakers, who are themselves thought leaders, share informative and interactive talks on their latest findings.
- People are highly encouraged to take breaks and power naps.
- A shared risk-taking environment supports people in buying into risk as a team.
- Clear and constructive feedback is given and further growth is fostered.

This is what I've discovered as a result of working with Losada's findings:

1. The 3:1 ratio of positivity definitely affects people and, as a consultant for various organisations, I've seen noticeably different levels of morale depending on where the firm stood in comparison to the ratio.

2. The 1 aspect of the ratio is critically important: high morale has to be based on both feet being firmly placed on solid ground.

Positive thinking has its advantages but also has its limitations. If it is used to cover up realistic evaluation, positive thinking becomes a hindrance. In my experience ignoring something that is real though undesired does not solve the issue. It keeps things at a superficial level.

It is vital to note that facing reality and making realistic evaluations is not to be confused with 'drama-driven negativity'. This robs us of creative energy. As an example, it does not take too much imagination to contrast the difference between when a person gives us constructive feedback and if the same person whines, moans and complains at us.

3. Positivity is best used when it acknowledges what is working as well as the growth that's still required. Communicating this in positive language stretches people and teams just enough to experience eustress. We know already that this is what triggers the parasympathetic nervous system which fills our brains with good chemicals. The opposite is distress where the sympathetic nervous system is triggered and fills our brain with the chemicals that trigger fight, flight, and freeze responses.

4. When working with the Losada Ratio, I became much more aware of the subtle positive messages that companies and organisations use even though they might not always be aware of the effect.

One great example that I recall is when an organisation that I had been contracted to for a project had a particularly strong focus on safety due to the high-risk nature of their construction-based industry in the oil and gas sector. Logic would dictate that the safety of people would be so logical that it wouldn't require additional motivation or incentives. To strive for excellence however, they tested out the idea of improving their already impressive safety performance by starting to make donations to local children's charities which would be linked to safety performance. If performance was poor or just good, donations were still made. When the statistics (usually monthly) showed that they were exceeding expectations, the donations were significantly increased. In addition, team members were randomly requested to take a turn and go and deliver the monthly cheques by hand so they could see with their own eyes the benefits the children experienced that resulted from working as safely as possible.

Attitudes towards safety became much more positive in a very natural way. It was as if the team effort towards a greater cause than themselves helped the individuals look after not just their own safety better, but also that of their colleagues. So a simple idea had a huge effect on the well-being of everyone involved.

5. I sometimes describe positivity as 'what works in favour of...' because positivity can be lost if you're trying to make something seem like its working when it's not. That's when positivity looks more like denial.

The following technique combines autopilot and automicity and is a helpful weekly recognition practice.

EXPERIENCE 10: ENGAGE WEEKLY RECOGNITION

Please fill in the table at the end of each week: Complete three examples of improvements you've made and just one example of an improvement you missed. I've included one of my weekly recognition lists to start you off.

Even the smallest of improvements are valuable when we compound concepts.

Please note that blank tables can be downloaded from http://www.findingthefulcrum.org.

Example: _Kieran O'Connor_ (name)

IMPROVEMENTS MADE THIS WEEK		IMPROVEMENTS MISSED THIS WEEK	
1	Two extra knuckle push-ups during Kung-Fu warms ups.	4	Didn't practice new Kung Fu footwork as planned this Sunday.
2	Went to bed earier than usual on two nights.		
3	Chatted with homeless guy rather than just giving him spare change.		

Example: _____ (name)

IMPROVEMENTS MADE THIS WEEK		IMPROVEMENTS MISSED THIS WEEK	
1		4	
2			
3			

For a lot of people, capturing four items out of a whole week might seem too little. If you want to have eight items or even 12, go ahead but please be mindful that it is wise to keep to a number which you will complete **each and every** week. Be gentle on yourself; let your subconscious take the reins.

When we complete a weekly LAS exercise, we recognise the progress we've made that week while also accepting that we didn't quite do everything that we would like to have done.

It uses the Losada Ratio to help switch on our RAS so it seeks out the numerous small improvements which make for natural motivation and, automatically, a better week.

You may or may not have noticed the Weekly Recognition format includes fractionation on the left-hand side (improvements made this week) which will help us maximise learnings. Our weekly perspective often sees things that we miss on a daily basis. Then we use defractionation as we cross over to the right-hand side (improvements missed this week). It helps us build overall discernment. It is important for our integrity that we acknowledge these items.

This weekly format recognises that people often see improvements as either too small to be worthwhile or too big to achieve. But it pays to remember:

> The journey of a thousand miles begins with one step.
>
> LAO TZU

All big successes are made up of lots and lots of small changes and successes - another example of the 'elusive obvious'. When we are happy with and grateful for even the smallest and simplest of improvements, we open ourselves up to more.

Do you remember Chapter 3.1 and Richard Wiseman's book *The Luck Factor?* This weekly practice will help utilise the power of your RAS to bring more of the good things in life to you. You earn it because you invest your time and effort wisely.

Monthly Reward

A study (Zadelius 2012) shared an interesting and useful finding: when people were promised a reward for a later task, they started to perform better at intermediate tasks even when they weren't subject to the reward. From this,

I made a simple cognition to create the quote at the start of this chapter so that I could firmly plant this understanding in my own subconscious:

 Reward yourself each month for a weekly task so that you will do better daily.

The monthly reward helps us keep going with the weekly recognition and the daily practice of LAS Lite™. This is a purist form of delayed gratification that helps create a high level of trust between your conscious and subconscious mind.

Another study (Lea and Wembly 2006) looked at the emotional charge of money when it's used as an incentive and came up with two theories about why it worked. First, we can perceive money as a tool to bring about the future we want through us being able to acquire what we desire. The second theory was that money has a similar effect on our brains as some drugs. Money used as a drug was linked to immediate gratification. When used a tool, it linked to delayed gratification. So money can be used as a tool that works to our benefit or it can be like a drug that is not so useful.

Another finding from Lea and Wembly was that virtual money didn't have anywhere near the same impact as cash and coins. Maybe this explains why my colleague felt such satisfaction as he watched the money mount up as he saved for his luxury watch. The subconscious likes things to be tangible; figures on a spreadsheet don't have the same effect as coins in a jar.

Some people prefer experiences to financial rewards. It all depends on the individual. For example, someone who is living on the breadline may be happier with cash whereas someone who is financially comfortable may be delighted by a small gift. I once gave a friend an aromatherapy massage gift voucher as she had helped me with a tricky project. I knew she loved being pampered but was working so hard that she needed some persuasion to take a break. A gift was enough leverage for her to make the time.

There will always be contexts about what makes a reward that really means something to us and is enough to make a difference for us as individuals. All I ask is that you test it out. Plan to give yourself a reward one month from now, one that 'works for you' over this time period so that your monthly, weekly and daily cycles all work with each other.

EXPERIENCE 11: ENGAGE MONTHLY REWARD

1. Tick the first table every day that you do your LAS Lite™ practice.
2. At the end of each week, tick the right line in box two if you did LAS Lite™ for five out of seven evenings or more (depending on the ratio you've set as your success score).
3. At the end of the month add up the days and work out the percentage for the month. If that figure meets or exceeds 80% (or whatever your target is) then you've earned yourself a reward!
4. I've included an example at the beginning to show you how the system works.

Example: *Kieran O'Connor* _____ (name)

PART 1: DAILY LAS LITE™ TICKLIST

1 ✓	2 ✓	3 ✓	4 ✓	5 ✓	6	7 ✓
8 ✓	9 ✓	10 ✓	11	12 ✓	13 ✓	14 ✓
15 ✓	16 ✓	17 ✓	18 ✓	19	20	21 ✓
22 ✓	23 ✓	24 ✓	25 ✓	26 ✓	27 ✓	28
29 ✓	30 ✓	31 ✓		% COMPLETED = *84%*		

PART 2: WEEKLY RECOGNITION TICKLIST

1 ✓	2 ✓	3 ✓	4 ✓	5 ✓	% COMPLETED = *100%*

PART 3: MONTHLY REWARD

A re-invigorating and relaxing Chinese acupressure massage | ✓

Example: _____ (name)

PART 1: DAILY LAS LITE™ TICKLIST

1	2	3	4	5	6	7
8	9	10	11	12	13	14
15	16	17	18	19	20	21
22	23	24	25	26	27	28
29	30	31	% COMPLETED =			

PART 2: WEEKLY RECOGNITION TICKLIST

1	2	3	4	5	% COMPLETED =

PART 3: MONTHLY REWARD

_____

The monthly reward is in five parts:

1. We select a reward to help us imagine how good it will be to achieve above the 80% level. Here we are creating the basis of a contract between conscious and subconscious.
2. We tick off LAS Lite™ at the end of each day.
3. We tick off weekly recognition each week.
4. At the end of the month, when we have achieved 80% or more, we celebrate.
5. Then we select a reward for the end of the next month.

You are free to change 80% as a measure of success to something that works better for you. I use 80% as it feels just right for me. It is challenging to do every day but it is not constraining.

Engaging A Yearly Picture

Towards the start of this book, I mentioned briefly how in years gone by, children would often have their height marked off on a wall chart. This was really important to them as parents could tell by their kids' bright smiles every time they witnessed even a little bit of growth. In the same way, a picture is always worth a thousand words to your subconscious mind. You can also ease and remove resistance by giving it irrefutable factual evidence just like the wall chart that measured children's growth.

EXPERIENCE 12: ENGAGE A YEARLY PICTURE

Example: *Kieran O'Connor* _____ (name)

1. At the end of each month, define what is the ratio of Eustress to Distress that you are generally experiencing.
2. Colour in the boxes to reflect your experience such that your overall total adds up to 100%.
3. I have included an example to get you started.

Note: There was a temporary drop in Month 8. This is a natural part of making progress. Hang in there, the subconscious will do its best to lure you back to distress often just when a big improvement is around the next corner.

Your yearly chart can be found below. If you don't want to fill in the one in this book, you can download examples from http://www.findingthefulcrum.org.

Example: _____ (name)

		1	2	3	4	5	6	7	8	9	10	11	12
% TIME IN EUSTRESS	100%												
	90%												
	80%												
	70%												
	60%												
	50%												
	40%												
	30%												
	20%												
	10%												
	0%												
% TIME IN DISTRESS	10%												
	20%												
	30%												
	40%												
	50%												
	60%												
	70%												
	80%												
	90%												
	100%												
	MONTH:	1	2	3	4	5	6	7	8	9	10	11	12

As you can see, all we do here is simply use the yearly chart to help record how we are doing monthly. There may be times where your balance between eustress/distress dips and so you may feel discouraged. In my experience, this is natural as we all go through ups and downs in life. Remember the snakes and ladders discussion? If you've just started a new job, you might find it takes a couple of months to settle into a new routine. Likewise, your eustress might rise because you had a fantastic vacation another month.

Be mindful that we are directing our communication to the subconscious here and not the conscious aspect of your mind.

Summary

- The Losada Ratio gives us a way to help train our minds to notice where we make improvements. This in turn leads to an environment where good luck is naturally earned.

- When we reward ourselves monthly for a weekly task, we do better daily.

- The subconscious likes to see data converted to symbolic format such as graphs and pictures.

In the next chapter we will wind up this journey and take a look at the far future.

"Study the past if you would divine the future."

CONFUCIUS

Aim Wrap things up by closing the loops that opened this book.

Concepts 1 Hofstadter's law.

Chapter 5.3

Leverage Your Future

Well here we are at the last chapter already. Before I go, I want to take you back to the time when you read the Introduction and three Daoist seeds were sown.

1. Separate and Combine
The Daoists were not just experts in learning but also in learning how to learn and they could see the elusive obvious - learning is a series of breaking things down and putting bits back together in a certain order. This book was constructed so that it incrementally offered you useful concepts. Actually I used them to write the book itself.

Over and over again, we have broken things down into simpler parts and put them back together again to help simplify the learning process. Now, whenever you get stuck, you'll veer away from acquiring more data and information and will be able to fall back on those concepts; practicing them will release your inner wisdom.

2. The Water Method
The Daoists describe two main methods of progressing in life: the fire method and the water method. The fire method is one where we impose force and struggle and we know it rather too well in the Western world. It has its place but it's not good to use it habitually as it compounds over time to create long-term distress.

The water method emphasises flow and following one's nature. In the Introduction, the sculptor respectfully and systematically chipped away at the parts of the stone that did not belong. This is what you may now be experiencing as you continue to practice LAS Lite™ each evening as well as the simple Weekly Recognition and Monthly Reward system. If you haven't experienced it yet, keep practicing! You will get there one step at a time. I suspect that you now have a greater understanding that there are some things common to us all such as how delayed gratification leads to more satisfaction. However, we are all as unique as our fingerprints and finding what works for you plus being open to how that can change like the tides will help you flow with life.

3. The Problem Isn't Where You Think It Is
As we have looked at leverage from various aspects, I hope that the idea of bringing balance to your life is now more tangible to you. The Western mindset is tuned into using force whenever we notice a problem and this is a little like shutting the door after the horse has bolted. With patience and the ideas around de-hypnosis within this book, you will have seen that most problems are not one-offs. They become noticeable only after a minimum of two occasions. With the ideas in here, you will be able to work towards balance much sooner. You will still have problems (we all have problems!), but you will have fewer of them and you'll be able to transcend them earlier and easier. This is not something that happens by magic; it is just that you are speaking the same language as your subconscious mind plus you are working to bring your conscious and subconscious into alignment.

Time: Friend Or Foe?

As the need for speed increases because of our technology-driven world, our time is being squeezed more and more. We try too hard to make things happen faster and follow the fire method route of attempting to force nature to follow our will. As the leverage of the subconscious to the conscious mind is about a million to one, this tells us how pointless applying force can be.

Hofstadter's Law:
Hofstadter's Law tells us that everything takes longer than you think it will. It's been useful knowing that, although I wish I'd understood it when I was a kid. I might not have had to be punished so often for late homework... I truly believed that even if I played football for just a little bit longer, I'd still be able to finish that easy-peasy essay. I guess denial is a habit that starts early.

Douglas Hofstadter, an American professor of the cognitive sciences, published his Pulitzer prize-winning book *An Eternal Golden Braid* in 1979. It explored how and why the human mind is so poor at estimating complex tasks. Hofstadter's Law says:

It always takes longer than you expect, even when you take Hofstadter's Law into account.

His studies helped clarify how we often underestimate tasks by associating them with work that is not as complex. Obvious as this may sound, what it does do is call the mind's reliability into question when it comes to planning deadlines and timing for complex projects. We know that when we plan tasks, such as home improvements, we tend to get a much more realistic timing for the start through to completion date when we break down the activities into those that can be done in parallel and those that can't.

Some have argued that we have an inbuilt desire to ignore facts at times. It's almost a form of denial when we intuitively feel that a job may take so long that even starting it is a bad idea so we overwhelm our minds with positivity in the form of baseless optimism.

There is a flip side. Landing man on the moon was questioned many times during the conception phase of the project but sheer determination won through. When you look back on this mammoth task, it was completed unbelievably quickly. It was as though the team had so little time to think that they didn't have time to doubt whether they would hit the deadline laid down by their countries president.

The main thing worth noting from Hofstadter's Law is to always be gentle with yourself if projects take longer than planned - while also taking full responsibility for those missed (often idealistic) deadlines. If you have a three-month timescale in your head to improve your life with leverage, give yourself a window of six to nine months. It's important that you align yourself with your eustress zone so that your timing wisely takes care of itself. This way you don't have to spend your time and energy fixing the problems you created along the way when you were experiencing the reactive mode of distress. The journey is always more important than the destination when you are learning how to learn.

Medium And Long-Term Strategies

In the UK, the government allows individuals to take advantage of an ISA (Individual Savings Account) where a certain sum of money can be invested. For example, for the tax year 2016/17 the ISA allowance is £15,240 per annum for cash, stocks and shares. The overwhelming majority of independent financial advisors will tell you that this is a perk that people should take advantage of if at all possible. They will also tell you that this is best suited to medium and longer term investments. This is why people who have taken full advantage since ISAs began in 1999 have seen the compounding effect now start to pay huge dividends - especially as this is all tax free. Everything gained in interest is compounded back in. This is what *The Little Book of Big Leverage* is designed to do.

Bringing Leverage Into Your Conscious Awareness

I thought it would be a good plan to share some ideas about leverage from this book which, as you'll recall, addressed both your conscious and your subconscious mind. Your subconscious steers your boat and your conscious is great at making minor course adjustments. When they work together, they allow you to take some control over your destination whatever your circumstances. I'll share just a sample of the leverage ideas that I applied when writing this book but without going into too much detail:

1. The word count is approximately 60,000 but also has 25 illustrations and experiences. Every picture is worth a thousand words to your subconscious mind so you could say that you've assimilated roughly about 85,000 words.

2. It was split into seven parts: -1, 0, 1, 2, 3, 4 and 5. I started with -1 and 0 as I wanted to create a strong foundation. Your subconscious will have recognised this even if you didn't consciously notice it.

3. I utilised many quotes to give additional support and authority.

4. I shared stories to activate the path between your conscious and subconscious so meanings were made on several levels in your mind.

5. The phrase 'what works for you' was repeated over and over again. This was part of the systematic practicing element.

6. Experiences were added for you to work through so you didn't just gain an intellectual understanding.

7. I added definitions for many keywords. Etymology allows you and your subconscious to make your own meanings. This helps make the subject matter more relevant to you.

8. I supported my ideas with scientific studies. Part of your mind is impressed by what other professional people and authorities think.

9. Chapters ended in what was coming next to prepare you for it. Some even jumped ahead where useful.

10. I purposely moved backwards and forwards within topics so that your conscious and subconscious fractionated (naturally learned) the material.

11. Worksheets were provided via my website so you have fewer reasons to skip the experiences.

12. LAS was hooked into our daily, weekly and monthly lives. LAS Lite™ is such an easy practice that it is harder not to do it.

13. This summary of leverage items is in itself leverage as your RAS is now seeking out other examples of leverage that I haven't covered in this list.

Last but not least:

14. I made it clear to my editor that I would only write this book if I did it by applying every leverage concept and principle that I share here. It's a kind of 'book writes itself' philosophy. I had to walk the talk before I could share my ideas with you.

Hopefully these 14 items give you a flavour of how leverage can be woven into your own life to create lasting improvements. There are many more and if you ever buy me a beer, I will gladly share lots of them with you. They are so enjoyable to discuss that I will no doubt have to buy you a beer back as it could take some time. It's difficult for me to stop talking about leverage once I get going.

Finishing The Story...

Remember the sculptor and the painter? It's time to finish their story. You thought the story was finished? Well, close but not quite.

So if you take your mind back, you will recall how the curious painter asked the sculptor how he did what he did and the sculptor said: "I don't create a sculpture as such. It's more that I uncover the form bit by bit" and went on to share:

Every block of stone has a statue inside it and it is the task of the sculptor to discover it.

MICHELANGELO

Well, the story didn't end there. The sculptor paused and said that paradoxically this was only half of the truth. He agreed with the great Michelangelo on yet another wise perception:

 The marble not yet carved can hold the form of every thought the greatest artist has.

The painter was bemused. "How can this be? The first quote says that the beauty is there no matter who the sculptor is, the second says the sculptor can influence what is sculpted. These are totally opposite ideas, aren't they?"

The sculptor paused for a moment, smiled mischievously, and said: "This is only true if black is truly the opposite of white. The reality of the universe is that there cannot be an outside without an inside, a left without a right, an up without a down."

He took a coin from his pocket, lifted it up to eye level and slowly rotated it back and forth to show and emphasise that the two sides were in fact part of one and the same coin. He placed the coin into the painter's hand and walked away to get on with his work leaving the painter pondering his words.

You may be wondering what on earth has this got to do with leverage and helping you work smarter so you do less of what doesn't work for you and more of what does. I am so pleased that you have such an enquiring mind!

Perplexingly, the block of stone has the potential within it, but it is the steady eye and hand of the sculptor that creates the actual final version. The former without the latter is positive thinking without the action. The latter without the former is misdirected effort.

Final Words

This book is the culmination of many years of research, study and real-world application into 'what works' generally for people and also what works for me as an individual. This two-level process helped me discover how to apply the water method in my own life by showing that we already have all the fundamental dynamics we need just ready to tap into, such as delayed gratification. However, we are all as unique as our own DNA and fingerprints. This is why this book is an open invitation for you to test the ideas and concepts that you find useful while leaving the others behind. Your choice completely.

I would like to take the opportunity to thank all the people whose quotes, research, findings, and feedback have inspired me and so much of this book. I owe you great thanks.

Before I go, I highly recommend that if you feel motivated to do so, reread this book in full several times, or at least the chapters that stood out most for you. To obtain and gain the most leverage, apply the ever-increasing intervals that align with Ebbinghaus's findings (see Chapter 3.3). After every repetition, the interval between reads gets longer as you will have absorbed more each time. The intervals want to be just enough to stretch your memory as you know now that your mind is designed to remember best just as you are about to forget. I hope you remembered to remember this. I am reminding you now just in case you didn't.

Joking aside... until next time, my fellow Natural Learner and Daily Discerner...

www.ingramcontent.com/pod-product-compliance
Lightning Source LLC
Chambersburg PA
CBHW071229080526
44587CB00013BA/1547